GLORIA COPELAND

GOD'S WILL

FOR
YOU

Expanded Legacy
EDITION

KENNETH
COPELAND
PUBLICATIONS

God's Will for You: Expanded Legacy Edition

ISBN 978-1-60463-207-1   30-0669

17 16 15 14 13 12   6 5 4 3 2 1

Kenneth Copeland Publications
Fort Worth, Texas 76192-0001

For more information about Kenneth Copeland Ministries, visit kcm.org or call 800-600-7395 (inside the U.S.) or 817-852-6000 (outside the U.S.).

CONTENTS

A Message From Kenneth Copeland

How can an individual definitely know God's will for his life? How do you get faith? I know God heals, but how do you get Him to do it? These and hundreds of questions like them are being asked in the hearts and minds of Christians all over the world. They are questions that cannot be answered by theology. They must be answered in the heart of the believer by the Holy Spirit of God from His written WORD.

Gloria and I began a search for the answers to these questions concerning faith when we accepted Jesus as LORD in 1962. We had to have some answers. We had just lost *everything* we had in a business venture that failed. The day Gloria turned her life over to Jesus, she was in a house almost completely empty of furnishings. I was out looking for a job. Like so many people, we knew there must be a better way, but *what was it?* Even after we became Christians, we were still continually in debt, sick much of the time and not at all effective witnesses for Jesus.

At the very beginning of our Christian lives, Gloria had a great desire for God's WORD. She read it even when she understood very little of what she was reading. She refused to quit searching. Then in 1967, in Tulsa, Oklahoma, we began to see that God's WORD is a living thing, and The WORD is the Father speaking personally to us. This was what God had been trying to teach us all the time, and soon, good things began happening. We started living in divine health, and God miraculously got us out of debt. Step by step, we were learning God's will for us.

This is not a book of theories, or ideas or traditions. It contains the priceless treasures that Gloria and I have learned about walking in faith and victory in Jesus. It is a book of *how to do it,* not just *you ought to do it.* One of the greatest faith men in the world said to me, "Kenneth, these are the steps to success: No. 1: Find out if it's God's will. No. 2: No longer confer with flesh and blood. No. 3: Get your job done at all costs."

This book will help you get started on the most important step— No. 1: *Find out God's will for you!*

—**Kenneth Copeland**

Introduction by Gloria Copeland

Kenneth was a commercial pilot and ex-nightclub singer when we got married. Neither of us knew The LORD. (I had always said, "Well, there is one thing I'll never do, and that's marry a preacher." Being married to a preacher was my idea of nothing to do, and Kenneth looked to be far from that when we married! At that time, my idea of preachers was not much, and even today, I'll have to admit, I've never met another man like him. We are still in love after 50 years—in fact, more so than ever!)

We had been married about six months when we decided to quit selling airplanes and work for a friend in a new business. I quit my job and went to work as their secretary. This looked like a promising venture, and we moved into a house on a lease-purchase agreement. We moved out of a furnished apartment, thinking that within a few days we could buy furniture. But within a few days, the new company was broke—and so were we!

We rented a rollaway bed for $7.50 a month. We had a coffee table and a television, which was the extent of our furnishings. One day, a neighbor came to the front door, and looking into the living room, asked, "Hasn't the moving van arrived?" All I could say was, "No, not yet!"

We were living in a three-bedroom house without even a refrigerator or a stove. We hardly had enough money to buy food. I cooked in an electric skillet and an electric coffeepot. As the weather began to get cold, I put a cardboard box on the porch to use as an icebox.

Once, I remember cooking a recipe of bananas fried in butter. It seems like I remember saying, "But, I thought you *liked* bananas!"

Our families did not know our situation. When we went to visit Kenneth's parents, it was a luxury to sit in a chair and to sleep in a bed that did not sag in the middle. His mother gave us a big sack of potatoes to take home. We went back to our empty, little house and ate potatoes for days—potatoes for breakfast, potatoes for lunch, potatoes for dinner. (I cooked them in my coffeepot.)

Ken was out most of the days looking for a job. I had a great deal of time and nothing to do. It certainly did not take me long to dust three pieces of furniture. I watched television until I almost climbed the walls. I made an effort to worry as much as possible, but that solved nothing. I was desperate. It looked as if there was nothing for me. The walls of my life had crumbled. The worst part of the situation was that I seemed helpless to do anything about it. In the past, I had always been able to think of some solution to almost any problem, but now, I had no answer.

At this point in my life, the light of The WORD of God flashed through the dark circumstances and became a reality to me. Under our coffee table was a New Testament written in everyday English that the Copelands had given Kenneth for his birthday. I picked it up and read the inscription at the front:

> Ken, Precious, Happy Birthday, today. "Seek ye first the kingdom of God, and his righteousness; and all these things shall be added unto you" (Matthew 6:33). With all our love, Mother and Daddy.

All these things shall be added unto you! I wanted to know more about that. I turned and began to read what Jesus said,

> Therefore I bid you put away anxious thoughts about food and drink to keep you alive, and clothes to cover your body. Surely life is more than food, the body more than clothes. Look at the birds of the air; they do not sow and reap and store in barns, yet your heavenly Father

feeds them. You are worth more than the birds! Is there
a man of you who by anxious thought can add a foot to
his height? And why be anxious about clothes? Consider
how the lilies grow in the fields; they do not work, they
do not spin; and yet, I tell you, even Solomon in all his
splendour was not attired like one of these. But if that
is how God clothes the grass in the fields, which is there
today, and tomorrow is thrown on the stove, will he
not all the more clothe you? How little faith you have!
No, do not ask anxiously, "What are we to eat? What
are we to drink? What shall we wear?" All these are
things for the heathen to run after, not for you, because
your heavenly Father knows that you need them all.
Set your mind on God's kingdom and his justice before
everything else, and all the rest will come to you as well.
So do not be anxious about tomorrow; tomorrow will
look after itself. Each day has troubles enough of its own
(Matthew 6:25-34, *The New English Bible*).

Suddenly, I realized that The LORD knew right where I was. The
food, the drink, the clothes were the things about which I had worried
and cried, and for which I had sought an answer. At the time, I thought
that material goods were about all that there was to life. It seemed that if
you were married to a man you loved, then financial prosperity should
bring happiness.

It is amazing how small our individual worlds are with no revelation
of God or His WORD. God, through His WORD, spoke to me on
a level I could understand. The wonderful, supernatural WORD has
the ability to meet each person on the level of his need. It is a personal

message from the Father to the one in need.

The Holy Spirit turned on a light inside me. I realized that God cared. He was already aware of my needs. The fact that He even took care of the birds was startling to me. On the same page I read, "Ask, and you will receive; seek, and you will find; knock, and the door will be opened. For everyone who asks receives, he who seeks finds, and to him who knocks, the door will be opened" (Matthew 7:7-8).

The truth began to make me free. I began to get a glimpse into the love of God. He cared! He really cared...even for me! He simply said ask, and I would receive. I got on my knees and asked Him to please do something with my life. I don't remember exactly what I prayed, but I do know that His WORD had caused faith to come into my heart, and I believed that He would give good things to me because of what His WORD said.

I did not realize what had happened to me spiritually until several months later. I did know that I wanted to read the Bible and had a desire to go to church. Jesus had said to set your mind on God's kingdom and all the rest will come to you. As far as I knew, I had begun to do that, but I knew nothing about spiritual things. I was raised in a church that did not teach the new birth or being born again. I didn't know that I had been born again until after I received the Holy Spirit.

But *God knew* and He began to move in my life. Within two weeks, Kenneth had a new job, we had a new car and a new apartment with new furniture. The WORD had already made me free from the kingdom of darkness and from the dire circumstances to which we had been bound. I had, in childlike faith, asked because of what I had seen in The WORD.

The day we moved into the new apartment, Ken called me into the living room and said, "What would you think if I started preaching or making talks about The LORD?" I remember thinking something like, *You must be kidding. You, preach? I can't even get you to go to church!* What I did not know until later was that The LORD had spoken to his heart that night, and Kenneth had done what he had been taught in a Baptist Sunday school years before. He had asked Jesus to come into his heart. I was living with a new man and didn't know it!

I had no traditions to hold me back and tell me why this good news was not for me. Although I had never attended church regularly, I had not questioned that there was a God. Jesus said it, and it never occurred to me not to believe Him. I believed the Bible was a Holy Book. I knew it had the Ten Commandments in it. I had a conscience that was quick to make me feel guilty, and I endeavored to obey it. But, I had never turned to Jesus and given Him the right to change me and my life.

In the past, I had tried to read the Bible because I knew that I should. If I struggled through one chapter, I thought that I had done my duty. The words that I read had no reality or revelation. But now, I had a hunger and desire to read The WORD. I loved it. I could not get enough of it. I was finding out about the God who is love. It was like being on a treasure hunt. I did not go back to work, and since I had no children, I spent my time reading The WORD. It was setting me free, just like Jesus said it would!

Three months later, we received the Holy Spirit. For five years, we plodded along spiritually, without knowing how to use our faith. We were so busy with our own problems, we didn't have time to help anyone else. We were controlled by our circumstances. We knew that we were born again and heaven would someday be our home, but we still lived very much the same way we had before we received the Holy Spirit. I continued to study The WORD, but without having received teaching, I didn't know enough to really walk in faith. We were still without money and still in debt. We didn't know any better than to be sick like everyone else. We believed in divine healing, but didn't know how to get it to work in our lives. We were not seeking first His kingdom, but our own.

I have told you about this nonproductive period in our lives to emphasize that receiving the Holy Spirit will not make you free. Jesus said that the truth would make you free. The Holy Spirit has come to teach and reveal The WORD to you. You will become free as you see these truths and *act on them.*

During those five years, nothing permanent worked out for us. We changed jobs frequently, but success was not to be ours. We tried everything we could think of and finally realized that *our* way was never going to work.

Ken knew he was called into the ministry of The LORD Jesus. It became clear to us that The LORD wanted him to go to Oral Roberts University. We thought about going to school for seven years and about our never-ending financial distress. We were reminded that Kenneth was 30 years old with a wife and two children. (Really three, but Ken's daughter Terri did not live with us.) Common sense told us that if we couldn't make a living working six days a week, then how could we even survive going to school? (Common sense will keep you bound to the world of the natural when it is time to step out in faith.)

It looked so impossible that we did not obey God for some time, but The LORD finally got through to us. We moved to Tulsa, Oklahoma, on faith and Kenneth started school. We were ready to do what God wanted. We began to walk by faith without knowing how, but we began to learn. The LORD took care of us. We set our minds on God's kingdom above everything else. All the rest has come to us, just as God's WORD promised it would.

For the first time in our Christian walk, we began to bear fruit as we learned to abide in Jesus and let His WORD live in us. The WORD you speak and act on is The WORD that is alive in you. We didn't know if we would be in school seven days or seven years. We didn't care. For the first time in our lives we were in God's will!

The first eight months we lived in Tulsa we knew very little about believing God for finances, but what we did know we believed with all our hearts, and we always had enough. The things we could not buy did not bother us. We were so thrilled with what was happening to us spiritually that material things seemed unimportant.

Kenneth was immediately assigned to Oral Roberts' airplane as co-pilot. This meant that he would go on every crusade and be in the middle of this great ministry of deliverance. He soon was assigned to work in the invalid room. He learned the ministry of praying for the sick from Oral Roberts—an education that only God could have provided.

If we had known that God was sending us to ORU for only one semester and that Kenneth would be put in a position to learn from Oral Roberts, personally, I am sure that we would not have been so slow to obey God. But, God desires that we obey Him in faith. Through The WORD and experience, we have learned that whatever God tells us to do is the most profitable thing for us—even though, in the natural, it might not look like it. We know now that He has planned the very best for our lives.

In the spring of 1967, The LORD spoke to Kenneth and commissioned him into the ministry of deliverance. We were in full-time ministry, at last, and The LORD began to open doors for Kenneth to preach His WORD.

In August of that year, we listened to a tape by Kenneth E. Hagin that revolutionized our lives. The name of it was *You Can Have What You Say.*[1] We studied and learned from him how to live—to be sustained—by our faith. We stayed in The WORD night and day until who we are in Christ became reality to us. As we learned the authority of The WORD, and began to act on what God says instead of the voice of tradition, circumstances and people, our lives were transformed.

In the past, we had mentally agreed that The WORD was true but did not know to act on it before we saw results. We weren't believing we received when we prayed. We only believed we received when the answer

---

1 Available through Kenneth Hagin Ministries, P.O. Box 50126, Tulsa, OK 74150-0126, or rhema.org.

came. Without The WORD living in us, we could only *hope* for results. We were hoping instead of believing in faith: Hope has no substance.

Faith is the substance of things hoped for. Faith comes by hearing The WORD. We learned that the Bible is His will for our lives, and we began to act on The WORD just as we would have if Jesus had spoken that WORD to us in person. As we became more accurate in operating The WORD of faith, results were inevitable.

We committed ourselves to put into practice whatever we saw in God's WORD. Some things changed immediately and others began to rapidly improve. Today, we are wholly dependent on God and His WORD to meet every need in our lives. "And my God will liberally supply...your every need according to His riches in glory in Christ Jesus" (Philippians 4:19, *The Amplified Bible*). God has supplied every need. We never lack any good thing. The truth has made us free from sickness, poverty, demons and fear.

This book is about what God's WORD will do in *your* life if you will obey Him. You can become the faith man or woman you have always longed to be. As you read, we believe you will be BLESSED, and the will of God for your life will become clear. Along with your reading, daily pray this prayer the Apostle Paul prayed for the Ephesian brethren. It is a Holy Spirit-inspired prayer and the will of the Father for you, personally, as well as for the Church, as a whole. You are asking for God's WORD— His will—to be revealed to you. It is written in the first person, just as you need to pray it. Set your faith to receive. We are standing with you for a revelation of *God's Will for You!*

> (LORD, I pray) that the God of our LORD Jesus
> Christ, the Father of glory, may give unto (me) the spirit
> of wisdom and revelation in the knowledge of him: the
> eyes of (my) understanding being enlightened; that (I)
> may know what is the hope of his calling, and what the

riches of the glory of his inheritance in the saints, and what is the exceeding greatness of his power to us-ward who believe, according to the working of his mighty power, which he wrought in Christ, when he raised him from the dead, and set him at his own right hand in the heavenly places, far above all principality, and power, and might, and dominion, and every name that is named, not only in this world, but also in that which is to come: and hath put all things under his feet, and gave him to be the head over all things to the church, which is his body, the fulness of him that filleth all in all (Ephesians 1:17-23).

GLORIA COPELAND

GOD'S WILL

FOR YOU

Expanded Legacy
EDITION

CHAPTER ONE

God's Will Is the New Birth

The will of God is revealed to us in His WORD. We can know the mind of God by His Spirit revealing His WORD—or His will—to us. Romans 12:2 says, "Be ye transformed by the renewing of your mind, that ye may prove what is that good, and acceptable, and perfect, will of God." We are transformed as we learn God's intention for our lives and act on that knowledge.

The Bible is God's testimony of what He has already prepared for His children. It is the Father teaching His family how to operate in His thoughts and His ways so that they can enjoy all that the lordship of Jesus offers.

The Bible is God speaking to you, now. God's WORD is alive. It is the living voice from heaven. You can fearlessly act on the written WORD of God, just as you would if Jesus called your name and spoke with you personally!

Faith is acting on The WORD of God in the same way you would act on the word of any honest man.

Jesus and His WORD are one. John 1:1, 14 says, "In the beginning was The WORD, and The WORD was with God, and The WORD was God.... And The WORD was made flesh, and dwelt among us." As you learn to make Jesus and His WORD LORD over your life, you will be successful in all that you do.

> FAITH IS ACTING ON THE WORD OF GOD IN THE SAME WAY YOU WOULD ACT ON THE WORD OF ANY HONEST MAN.

To be transformed, as Romans 12:2 instructs us, your mind must be renewed to the will of God for you! God has made available, through His written WORD, the avenue through which we may be transformed, learn the exact knowledge of Him and how to operate in His higher ways. (Read Isaiah 55.)

The renewing of the mind brings the will into agreement with the Father's will. As we fill our minds with His WORD, we then begin to think as He thinks, and His ways become our ways. We become, through His power and wisdom, a master of the circumstances of life.

It is God's perfect will for *all* men to be saved and to come into the knowledge of the truth (1 Timothy 2:3-4). Peter tells us that God is not willing that any should perish. Not only is it His will for you to be saved, but it is also His will for you to be free so you can discern and walk in "that good, and acceptable, and perfect, will of God" for you (Romans 12:2).

The Father desires that His children be free now and live victoriously over the evil caused by Satan. He wants you to do His WORD because it works deliverance for you. Jesus said, "Ye shall know the truth, and the truth shall *make* you free" (John 8:32). "Thy WORD is truth" (John 17:17).

ADAM'S AUTHORITY

As we investigate The WORD of God in the light of our redemption by Christ Jesus, we see to what great lengths the Father went in order to bring man back into union with Him after the Fall of Adam. John 3:16 says, "For God so loved the world, that he gave his only begotten Son, that whosoever believeth in him should not perish, but have everlasting life." God gave His only begotten Son in the form of man, born of a virgin, because of the sin of high treason Adam (God's man) had committed in the Garden of Eden.

Adam was created in God's image. Adam and Eve were righteous and could fellowship with God. They were not acquainted with evil. God had made them to succeed—not to fail.

God gave His man authority and dominion over every living creature, including Satan: "And God BLESSED them, and God said unto them, Be fruitful, and multiply, and replenish the earth, and subdue it: and have dominion over the fish of the sea, and over the fowl of the air, and over every living thing that moveth upon the earth" (Genesis 1:28).

Adam had the God-given ability to rule the earth. God placed in his hands unlimited power over this world. The earth was Adam's to oversee. He was to rule the earth as God rules heaven, and by the same spiritual laws and power. Even though he was given dominion, that dominion was to be enforced according to the Father's will. He was God's underruler.

ADAM'S DEFEAT

"And The LORD God commanded the man, saying, Of every tree of the garden thou mayest freely eat: But of the tree of the knowledge of good and evil, thou shalt not eat of it: for in the day that thou eatest thereof thou shalt surely die" (Genesis 2:16-17).

The serpent beguiled Eve. She ate and, just as God had said, she died. First Timothy 2:14 tells us that the woman was deceived, but the man was not. Adam saw that his fellowship with Eve was gone. *The great gulf of spiritual death had separated them.* He chose to disobey God and to be one with Eve. This was Adam's great sin—high treason against God. Fully aware that it would mean separation from God, he ate.

God had said, "For in the day that thou eatest thereof thou shalt surely die." Yet, we see that Adam lived hundreds of years longer, physically. Romans 5:12 reveals how Adam fulfilled this word the same day that he ate, "Wherefore, as by one man sin entered into the world, and death by sin; and so death passed upon all men, for that all have sinned." God's warning to Adam was speaking of spiritual death—the sin nature. That day in the Garden, first Eve, then Adam changed gods. The sin nature of their new god, Satan, took possession of their once righteous spirits that day, and *they died spiritually.* The very nature of man was changed from one of righteousness, or eternal life, into one of spiritual death—from the nature of God to the nature of Satan. From that day forward, spiritual death began its reign over mankind.

Spiritual law decrees that every living thing brings forth after its own kind. Adam and Eve were the parents of all human life and, so, from then on, by them, their now sin nature was born into all men. This spiritual death eventually brought physical death. If Adam had not died spiritually, he would never have died physically.

God had created Adam a righteous, eternal man, but sin separated him from his Creator. It is not punishment from God that alienates a man from the family of God, but the sin nature with which the man is born. Hell was not created for man but for the devil and his angels. Satan is taking men there with him (Matthew 25:41).

Adam gave his authority into the hands of a merciless ruler and took on the nature of his new god—the devil. Satan is called the god of this world (2 Corinthians 4:4). Adam was born again from life to death, the nature of his new god. God had given complete authority to His man Adam, so it was Adam's to give away (Genesis 1:26).

Thousands of years later, when the devil took Jesus to the top of a high mountain and showed Him all the kingdoms of the world and their glory, Satan reminded Jesus of Adam's treason. Satan said, "To You I will give all this power and authority and their glory...for it has been turned over to me, and I give it to whom I will" (Luke 4:6, *The Amplified Bible*).

Jesus knew well that Satan did have the power and authority over it, for He said, "Get thee behind me, Satan" (verse 8).

As we realize the state mankind is in because of Adam's high treason, we can, for the first time, see why Jesus had to come in the flesh and be born of a virgin.

Satan thought he had man forever in his power. Never, in his selfish nature, could he see that God would suffer at His own hand to get man back. Satan could not begin to comprehend the love of God. He never dreamed God would sacrifice His only Son in order to free man.

MAN'S REDEMPTION

God had created man for fellowship. His desire for a family was so great that He sent His only begotten Son into this world to be man's substitute. No one else could have qualified. It had to be the righteous for the unrighteous (1 Peter 3:18).

Now, do you see the necessity of the virgin birth? The Savior of the world could not be born of a sin-natured man. He had to be the righteousness of God in order to bear the penalty for man's sin, yet He also had to be a man. "But when the fulness of the time was come, God sent forth his Son, made of a woman...that we might receive the adoption of sons" (Galatians 4:4-5).

A man had been the key figure in the Fall, so a man had to be the key figure in the redemption. "For since [it was] through a man that death [came into the world, it is] also through a Man that the resurrection of the dead [has come]. For just as [because of their union of nature] in Adam all people die, so also [by virtue of their union of nature] shall all in Christ be made alive" (1 Corinthians 15:21-22, *The Amplified Bible*).

As the Holy Spirit hovered over Mary, there was conceived in her a "holy thing." "And the angel answered and said unto her, The Holy Ghost shall come upon thee, and the power of the Highest shall over-shadow thee: therefore also that holy thing which shall be born of thee shall be called the Son of God" (Luke 1:35).

Because God was, literally, the Father of the child to be born of Mary, Jesus was brought into this world a righteous man, out from under the rule and dominion of Satan. Jesus said the prince of this world (Satan) had nothing in Him (John 14:30).

YOUR SUBSTITUTE

Jesus, the only Son of God, stripped Himself of His heavenly privi-leges and became like men (Philippians 2:7, *The Amplified Bible*). He took upon Himself flesh.

No wonder Satan has attacked and tried to undermine the reality of the virgin birth! Without the righteousness of God in a man, there could have been no substitute to secure our release from Satan's dominion.

It is God's will for you to be saved and to know the truth of what Jesus purchased for you. Jesus went to the cross as *your substitute,* paying the price for Adam's sin. He suffered in His own body, and more impor-tantly, in His spirit. He experienced the same spiritual death that entered man in the Garden of Eden. Second Corinthians 5:21 says, "For he hath made him to be sin for us, who knew no sin; that we might be made the righteousness of God in him."

Jesus became one with man in spiritual death to make it possible for us to become one with Him in eternal life. He never committed one sin, but was *made* sin, and then suffered sin's penalty for us.

And he made his grave with the wicked, and with the
rich in his death; because he had done no violence,
neither was any deceit in his mouth. Yet it pleased The
LORD to bruise him; he hath put him to grief: when
thou shalt make his soul an offering for sin, he shall see
his seed, he shall prolong his days, and the pleasure of
The LORD shall prosper in his hand. He shall see of the
travail of his soul, and shall be satisfied: by his knowledge shall my righteous servant justify many; for he shall
bear their iniquities. Therefore will I divide him a portion with the great, and he shall divide the spoil with the
strong; because he hath poured out his soul unto death:
and he was numbered with the transgressors; and he bare
the sin of many, and made intercession for the transgressors (Isaiah 53:9-12).

After Jesus was made sin, He had to be born again from spiritual
death to spiritual life: "God hath fulfilled the same unto us their children, in that he hath raised up Jesus again; as it is also written in the second psalm, Thou art my Son, this day have I begotten thee" (Acts 13:33).

What day? The first part of the verse explains "this day" as the day
God raised Jesus from the dead. God raised Him up and liberated Him
from the pains of death. Jesus was made alive—or justified—in the spirit.
(1 Timothy 3:16; Acts 2:24; 1 Peter 3:18, *The Amplified Bible).* Once
again, He was the righteousness of God and, once again, eternal life was
His nature.

Let the picture of the firstborn from among the dead become a
reality in your spirit and mind. Jesus was not only a being with God's
nature and Spirit, but also the *man* who said, "Behold my hands and my
feet, that it is I myself: handle me, and see; for a spirit hath not flesh and

bones, as ye see me have" (Luke 24:39). First Timothy 2:5 says of Him, "For there is one God, and one mediator between God and men, the *man* Christ Jesus." Jesus is a born-again *man*. He came from death back into life. (This is the same new birth that the good news of the gospel still offers to any man who will accept it!)

Jesus was changed from having been made sin, into a new creature, so righteous that He was able to present Himself before the Father, once again, the spotless Son of God. As He went, He opened the way for you to have full freedom and confidence to enter into the presence of the Father through Him. Jesus said, "I am the way, the truth, and the life: no man cometh unto the Father, but by me" (John 14:6).

By Jesus, any man can come!

The Church came into existence when Jesus became the first to be born from the dead. "And he is the head of the body, the church: who is the beginning, the firstborn from the dead; that in all things he might have the preeminence" (Colossians 1:18). Only in the four Gospels and Acts is Jesus spoken of as the only begotten Son. Now, He is the firstborn among many brethren: "For whom he did foreknow, he also did predestinate to be conformed to the image of his Son, that he might be the firstborn among many brethren" (Romans 8:29).

You have to grasp the reality of Jesus taking your place in order to see what He has made available in the new birth to you and to whosoever will. Jesus opened the way for the world—every man—into the Father's family! The Father offers *you* the opportunity to be made like His firstborn, The LORD Jesus Christ.

Two Families

There are two families operating in the world today. We have seen the one that began with Adam's treason when spiritual death spread to all men. Ephesians 2:3 tells us that we were by nature the children of wrath, even as others. "That at that time ye were without Christ, being aliens

> JESUS OPENED
> THE WAY FOR YOU TO
> ENTER INTO
> THE PRESENCE
> OF THE FATHER
> THROUGH HIM.

from the commonwealth of Israel, and strangers from the covenants of promise, having no hope, and without God in the world" (verse 12).

First John 3:10 speaks of the other family, the children of God, and the children of the devil. "In this the children of God are manifest, and the children of the devil: whosoever doeth not righteousness is not of God, neither he that loveth not his brother."

Every person belongs to one family or the other. You must be reborn, out of the family of Satan, just as by natural birth you were born into it. In John 3:5-6, Jesus said, "Verily, verily, I say unto thee, Except a man be born of water and of the Spirit, he cannot enter into the kingdom of God. That which is born of the flesh is flesh; and that which is born of the Spirit is spirit."

All of us were born physically—or of the flesh—into the family of the devil because of Adam's sin. We were, by nature, the children of wrath, without God in the world. To get into the kingdom, or family, of God, Jesus said *you must be born over again.*

You cannot work to deserve this family or gradually grow into it. You must be *born* into it. When a person is shown why he needs to be born again, he will want deliverance out of Satan's family and entry into the family of God, the Father.

Satan is a merciless, cruel ruler, but the Father is the God of love. Satan, the thief, came to steal, kill and destroy. Jesus came that we might have life and have it more abundantly (John 10:10).

WHAT MUST I DO TO BE BORN AGAIN?

Romans 10:9-10 says, "That if thou shalt confess with thy mouth The

LORD Jesus, and shalt believe in thine heart that God hath raised him from the dead, thou shalt be saved. For with the heart man believeth unto righteousness; and with the mouth confession is made unto salvation."

To be made a new creature in Christ, confess, or say, with your mouth Jesus is LORD and believe in your heart that God has raised Him from the dead, and you will be saved. You have God's WORD for it.

When you do this, you are changing lords. In the past, you were lorded over by the devil, but today, you are making Jesus LORD over your life!

Say this out loud:

> Jesus, I make You LORD over my life. I repent of sin. I turn from sin and follow You. I believe in my heart that God raised You from the dead. I give myself to You. This day, I confess You as LORD. Therefore, according to Your WORD, I am saved! Thank You for making me new and for giving me eternal life.

Now, speak to your new Father:

> Father, I am a new creature in Christ. Fill me with Your Holy Spirit to enable me to be a powerful witness for Jesus. I believe that I now receive the Holy Spirit, just as the disciples did on the Day of Pentecost.

Romans 10:10 tells us that with the heart man believes to righteousness and with the mouth confession is made to salvation. The moment you made Jesus LORD over your life, the Holy Spirit created in you a new spirit—one that is born in the image of Jesus.

You are made the righteousness of God. The day you are born again, you are as righteous as you will ever be. It is not something that you attain or earn, but a free gift. "For if by one man's offence death reigned by one; much more they which receive abundance of grace and of the gift of righteousness shall reign in life by one, Jesus Christ" (Romans 5:17).

THE NEW CREATURE

"Therefore if any man be in Christ, he is a new creature: old things are passed away; behold, all things are become new. And all things are of God.... For he hath made him to be sin for us, who knew no sin; that we might be made the righteousness of God in him" (2 Corinthians 5:17-18, 21).

Jesus said that which is born of the Spirit is spirit. Your spirit has literally been born again. You are made new on the inside—a new creature—a new species of being. This new man never existed before.

One writer describes the new creature as something that has just been spoken into existence, like a new star, a full-grown tree or a newly built house. God reproduces Himself in the new creature. You have been made a son of the living God by His own Holy Spirit.

First Peter 3:18, *The Amplified Bible,* tells us that Jesus was made alive in the spirit. Compare this scripture with what happens to us in Ephesians 2:5 from the same version: "He made us alive together in fellowship and in union with Christ; [He gave us the very life of Christ Himself, the same new life with which He quickened Him]."

You have the same new life with which God quickened—or made alive—Jesus!

Instead of the sin nature man has when he enters this world, the new creature has the nature of God Himself. Old things have passed away. There are no yesterdays from the time you make Jesus LORD over your life. Spiritual death and sin are eradicated from you, and the nature of God—eternal life—is put in. You are a twice-born man. You belong to God's family.

You have been delivered out of the kingdom of darkness and

translated into the kingdom of God's dear Son (Colossians 1:13). Satan can no longer lord it over you, unless you allow it. He is no longer your god, but Jesus is LORD over your life. Jesus Himself said, "All power is given unto me in heaven and in earth" (Matthew 28:18).

There is no doubt that when you receive Jesus as LORD of your life, you are on the winning side. The life you now live in this body, you live by faith in the Son of God. You need no longer be bound by fear, poverty, sickness or Satan. *You are free!*

THE NAME OF JESUS

The Name of Jesus is now yours to use. His Name carries authority in three realms: in heaven, on earth and under the earth. Philippians 2:10 says, "That at the name of Jesus every knee should bow, of things in heaven, and things in earth, and things under the earth." With this mighty Name, you are now able to stand against the wiles of Satan and restrain his evil works in your life and in the lives of others. You are more than a conqueror. You are a Christian.

Jesus tells you, in His Name, to cast out the devil (Mark 16:17). You can quickly recognize the work of the adversary. Doubt, discouragement and defeat are from Satan.

When you meet with temptation, dare to boldly use the Name of Jesus, and cast the devil out of your situation, whatever it may be. James 4:7 says, "Resist the devil, and he will flee from you." He has to flee at the Name of Jesus, spoken in faith, from the lips of a believer. Speak directly to the enemy and say, "Satan, I resist you. In the Name of Jesus I command you to get out." (Be specific in your command.)

Jesus stripped Satan of all his power when He was raised from the dead. He then gave this power to His Church to use on earth. "And he said unto them, Go ye into all the world, and preach the gospel to every creature.... And these signs shall follow them that believe; In my name shall they cast out devils; they shall speak with new tongues; they

> FROM THE MOMENT YOU MAKE JESUS LORD, YOU HAVE ETERNAL LIFE ABIDING IN YOU.

shall take up serpents; and if they drink any deadly thing, it shall not hurt them; they shall lay hands on the sick, and they shall recover" (Mark 16:15, 17-18).

Jesus already had authority over the devil. He proved that at every turn during His ministry on earth. He didn't need to get authority for Himself—He got it for you.

It is up to you to enforce this authority in your life with the Name of Jesus and The WORD of God. In Jesus, and by His Name, the newest Christian has authority over Satan.

Confessing Jesus as LORD is the greatest and most important step in God's will for your life. If you do not act on Romans 10:9-10, and make Jesus LORD over your life, this book will be of no value to you. Without the lordship of Jesus, you have no access to the Father. The perfect will of God can function only in the lives of believers.

Let there be no doubt in your mind that from the moment you make Jesus LORD, you have eternal life abiding in you. First John 5:11-13 tells us, "And this is the record, that God hath given to us eternal life, and this life is in his Son. He that hath the Son hath life; and he that hath not the Son of God hath not life. These things have I written unto you that believe on the name of the Son of God; that ye may know that ye have eternal life, and that ye may believe on the name of the Son of God."

When you receive Jesus as LORD, you are stepping into the beginning of God's perfect will for your life. Know that you now have eternal life. You are a saved person. You are a new creature in Christ Jesus. You are no longer to identify with sin but with righteousness!

WATER BAPTISM

Even so consider yourselves also dead to sin and your
relation to it broken, but [that you are] alive to God
[living in unbroken fellowship with Him] in Christ
Jesus. Let not sin therefore rule as king in your mortal
(short-lived, perishable) bodies, to make you yield
to their cravings and be subject to its lusts and evil
passions. Do not continue offering or yielding your
bodily members [and faculties] to sin as instruments
(tools) of wickedness. But offer and yield yourselves to
God as though you have been raised from the dead to
[perpetual] life, and your bodily members [and faculties]
to God, presenting them as implements of righteousness.
For sin shall not [any longer] exert dominion over
you, since now you are not under Law [as slaves], but
under grace [as subjects of God's favor and mercy]
(Romans 6:11-14, *The Amplified Bible*).

In the book of Acts, we see that new converts were baptized in water.
Water baptism is a physical act testifying to the miracle that took place
inside you when you made Jesus LORD. It is to be used as a point of contact to help you release your faith and mentally grasp what happened to
you on the inside. As you are raised from the water, see yourself through
the eye of faith. Consider yourself dead to sin and alive to God, living in
unbroken fellowship with Him—in Christ Jesus. You are presenting your
body a living sacrifice, holy, acceptable unto God, which is your reason-
able service (Romans 12:1).

Exercise your will, and determine that sin shall no longer exert dominion over you.

Your Advocate With the Father

If you sin after you have become a new man in Christ, 1 John 1:9 gives instructions on how to receive forgiveness: "If we confess our sins, he is faithful and just to forgive us our sins, and to cleanse us from all unrighteousness." And, 1 John 2:1 says, "My little children, these things write I unto you, that ye sin not. And if any man sin, we have an advocate with the Father, Jesus Christ the righteous."

Act on this scripture immediately, and let nothing interfere in your fellowship with your Father. If you confess your sins, you have His WORD that He will forgive and cleanse you from all unrighteousness.

Hebrews 10:17 tells us when God forgives, He forgets. Use your faith, and see yourself forgiven. You have made it right with God, and your fellowship has been restored. Jesus has upheld you, and there is nothing standing between you and the Father. You have confessed your sin, and now you go free.

When you realize you have sinned, be quick to confess wrongdoing and get rid of it. Stay in close fellowship with the Father and The LORD Jesus.

Prayer Privileges

John 17:23 tells us that the Father loves you even as He loves Jesus. You are His son and He is your Father. Because of this, you are invited to come boldly to the throne of grace and obtain mercy and find grace to help in time of need (Hebrews 4:16).

John 16:23 assures us that, "In that day ye shall ask me nothing. Verily, verily, I say unto you, Whatsoever ye shall ask the Father in my name, he will give it you" (John 16:23).

Pray to the Father, in the Name of Jesus, and lay your petition before the throne of grace. Use John 16:23 in prayer, and expect to get results.

"And this is the confidence that we have in him, that, if we ask any thing according to his will, he heareth us: And if we know that he hear us, whatsoever we ask, we know that we have the petitions that we desired of him" (1 John 5:14-15).

"And whatsoever we ask, we receive of him, because we keep his commandments, and do those things that are pleasing in his sight" (1 John 3:22).

Prayer that brings results must be based on God's WORD. Find the scriptures that promise the things you desire, and you'll have the assurance that you are asking according to His will! *God's WORD is His will for you.* Basing your prayer on God's WORD causes faith to rise up on the inside of you to grasp the answer and leaves no room for doubt.

The next step is to believe you receive your petition. The WORD says, "Therefore I say unto you, What things soever ye desire, when ye pray, believe that ye receive them, and ye shall have them" (Mark 11:24).

You are to believe you receive when you pray. From that moment, you are not to be moved by what you see, even though circumstances may look contrary to the answer. You must hold fast to your confession of faith until your desire comes to pass in the natural realm.

Faith is believing God's WORD, regardless of what you see.

This operation of faith in God's WORD releases His power to change your circumstances, heal your body and provide for you supernaturally.

As you hold fast to your confession of faith, continue to give praise and thanksgiving to the Father for the manifestation of the answer. Because it is written in The WORD you know you have it. Consider it done!

YE SHALL BE WITNESSES UNTO ME

Your life has been changed and you have been made free. Now, go and share Jesus with someone else! God wants you to be an instrument He can use to deliver others. You were "...created in Christ Jesus unto good works" (Ephesians 2:10). To be His instrument is the privilege of every born-again child of God.

You have learned from the Bible how to make Jesus LORD and be made new on the inside. Tell your friends, neighbors and family what Jesus has done for you. Share with them the scriptures that gave you new life. Be a witness to them that Jesus is LORD and alive today to meet *their* needs!

Give The WORD of life!

SCRIPTURE:

"For this is good and acceptable in the sight of God our Saviour; who will have all men to be saved, and to come unto the knowledge of the truth" (1 Timothy 2:3-4).

POINTS TO REMEMBER:

1. The Bible is God speaking to you now. The WORD is alive. It is the living voice from heaven. You can fearlessly act on the written WORD of God just as you would if Jesus called your name and spoke with you personally.

2. To be made a new creature in Christ, confess, or say, with your mouth Jesus is LORD and believe in your heart that God has raised Him from the dead, and you will be saved. You have God's WORD for it.

3. You have been delivered out of the kingdom of darkness and translated into the kingdom of God's dear Son (Colossians 1:13). Satan can no longer lord it over you, unless you allow it. He is no longer your god, but Jesus is LORD over your life.

CONFESSION:

I make Jesus The LORD of my life. I believe He died for me and was raised from the dead for me. I confess Him as my Savior and LORD. I declare by faith that I am a new creation in Christ Jesus. Old things are passed away, and all things have become new in my life with Jesus. Sin no longer has dominion over me. I am created in God's image, and I am free from sin. I am forgiven. I believe, according to John 17:23, that the Father loves me as much as He loves Jesus. I receive His love for me.

God's WORD is life to me, and I put it first place in all I do. I believe I receive the Holy Spirit, just as the disciples did on the Day of Pentecost. I step into God's perfect plan for my life, and I rejoice that eternal life is abiding in me. The powerful, overcoming Name of Jesus is mine, and I use it to live an overcoming life of faith in my LORD Jesus!

CHAPTER TWO

God's Will Is the Holy Spirit

Yου have been involved with the Holy Spirit since you first heard the good news that Jesus took your place and bore the penalty for your sins. It was the Holy Spirit, through The WORD, who made the truth that Jesus was raised from the dead a reality in your heart. First Corinthians 12:3 states that no man can even say Jesus is LORD except by the Holy Ghost.

Jesus came to make it possible for man to receive the nature of God—eternal life (John 10:10). Jesus could not get a man born again while He was on the earth. He had the power to forgive sins, but there could be no new creatures until Jesus paid the sin price at Calvary and became the firstborn from the dead.

> Nevertheless I tell you the truth; It is expedient for you
> that I go away: for if I go not away, the Comforter will
> not come unto you; but if I depart, I will send him unto

you.... I have yet many things to say unto you, but ye cannot bear them now. Howbeit when he, the Spirit of truth, is come, he will guide you into all truth: for he shall not speak of himself; but whatsoever he shall hear, that shall he speak: and he will show you

IT WAS THE HOLY SPIRIT, THROUGH THE WORD, WHO MADE THE TRUTH THAT JESUS WAS RAISED FROM THE DEAD A REALITY IN YOUR HEART.

things to come. He shall glorify me: for he shall receive of mine, and shall show it unto you. All things that the Father hath are mine: therefore said I, that he shall take of mine, and shall show it unto you (John 16:7, 12-15).

Jesus told the men who walked by His side for three years that it was more profitable for them if He went away and sent the Holy Spirit to them.

It is the miraculous work of the Holy Spirit that makes you a new creature. When you make Jesus LORD over your life, the Holy Spirit comes upon you and overshadows you, just as He did Mary when there was conceived in her a "holy thing" (Luke 1:35).

Spiritual death is then eradicated from your spirit. You are born again into a new life—a new spirit. You are literally born of God. "Beloved, *now* are we the sons of God" (1 John 3:2). "Whosoever believeth that Jesus is the Christ is born of God" (1 John 5:1). God becomes your Father by spiritual birth.

The miracle of the new birth should never become commonplace to you. It is not a theological idea, but a fact. The Holy Spirit personally carries out this miracle when you make Jesus Christ your LORD. He takes a sin-ridden, selfish man and re-creates his spirit in God's image. This change in a man's nature is a great, miraculous and supernatural event in the realm of the spirit. This is why all of heaven rejoices (Luke 15:7, 10).

THE SPIRIT WITHIN

The ministry of the Holy Spirit is not only to impart the nature of God to the spirit of man, but also to live in the new creature and to reveal to him the exact knowledge of God. The Spirit within enables the new creature to walk in newness of life. He gives us this life, and He also sustains it.

Ezekiel says, "A new heart also will I give you, and a new spirit will I put within you: and I will take away the stony heart out of your flesh, and I will give you an heart of flesh. And I will put my spirit within you, and cause you to walk in my statutes, and ye shall keep my judgments, and do them" (Ezekiel 36:26-27).

After you make Jesus your LORD, the Holy Spirit comes to live inside you. Jesus told the disciples: "If ye love me, keep my commandments. And I will pray the Father, and he shall give you another Comforter, that he may abide with you for ever; even the Spirit of truth; whom the world cannot receive, because it seeth him not, neither knoweth him: but ye know him; for he dwelleth with you, and *shall be in you*" (John 14:15-17). The Holy Spirit had been working with the disciples and they had been preaching, healing the sick and casting out devils. He had been with them and working with them, but Jesus said when the Holy Spirit came to stay with them forever, He would live on the inside of them. He told them, "Peace be unto you: as my Father hath sent me, even so send I you. And when he had said this, he breathed on them, and saith unto them, Receive ye the Holy Ghost" (John 20:21-22).

After Jesus had been raised from the dead, He appeared to the disciples and they were born again as Jesus breathed the life of God into them, saying, "Receive the Holy Spirit." (Compare with Genesis 2:7.)

Eternal life came into them. They could not have been born again until after Jesus paid the price for sin. As they received the life of God, the Spirit who gave that life began to dwell in them.

THE SPIRIT UPON

From that moment, the disciples were changed. They were no longer troubled, afraid or sad. Luke's account lets us know of the change: "And it came to pass, while he BLESSED them, he was parted from them, and carried up into heaven. And they worshipped him, and returned to Jerusalem with great joy: and were continually in the temple, praising and blessing God. Amen" (Luke 24:51-53).

Where there had been sadness, now there was great joy—a fruit of the spirit. Where there was fear and confusion, now there was continual praise and blessing of God. And, they were obedient. They went to Jerusalem to wait for yet another wonderful event to come that Jesus had promised before He was carried into heaven—the enduement of power from on high. Jesus had told them, "And, behold, I send the promise of my Father upon you: but tarry ye in the city of Jerusalem, until ye be endued with power from on high" (verse 49).

Acts 1:4-5, 8 says:

> And, being assembled together with them, commanded them that they should not depart from Jerusalem, but wait for the promise of the Father, which, saith he, ye have heard of me. For John truly baptized with water; but ye shall be baptized with the Holy Ghost not many days hence.... But ye shall receive power, after that the Holy Ghost is come upon you: and ye shall be witnesses unto me both in Jerusalem, and in all Judaea, and in Samaria, and unto the uttermost part of the earth.

He said they were to be baptized with the Holy Ghost and receive power! They had already received the Holy Spirit within. Now, Jesus was instructing them what to do to receive the power of God *upon* them. Acts 10:38 says Jesus was anointed with the Holy Ghost and power, and now the disciples were to receive that same power.

In our everyday language, He said, "Don't leave town without it!" This enduement of power was necessary to carry out the work Jesus set before them. (See Mark 16:15-20; Matthew 28:18-20.) Nothing has changed. The Body of Christ today is still under the same mandate.

Jesus taught the disciples about this in John 14. He talked to them about the Holy Spirit and said, "Believest thou not that I am in the Father, and the Father in me? the words that I speak unto you I speak not of myself: but the Father that dwelleth in me, he doeth the works.... Verily, verily, I say unto you, He that believeth on me, the works that I do shall he do also; and greater works than these shall he do; because I go unto my Father" (verses 10, 12).

They were to continue to do the same works Jesus Himself had been doing, with His power and Anointing that had come on them and the Church on the Day of Pentecost. (See Acts 2:1-21, 5:12-16, 10:38; Matthew 3:16-17; Luke 4:18-21; John 14:10.)

The Holy Spirit is still assigned to the Church to help us fulfill our commission. Didn't Jesus say He would abide with us forever? (See John 14:16.)

Jesus said that it was not Him, but the Father in Him, who did the works. When He said, "But ye shall receive power, after that the Holy Ghost is come upon you" (Acts 1:8), they knew what He meant!

The Greek word *dunamis,* translated *power,* means "ability and might." When you receive the Baptism in the Holy Spirit, you receive the ability of God to do His work in the earth. The Spirit within us is for fruit bearing—for our own personal lives (Galatians 5:22-23). Jesus talked about this in John 4:14. He called it: "...a well of water springing up into everlasting life." But the Spirit *upon* is for service. He described it in John 7:38-39 as rivers of living water. The well is for your own life, and the rivers flowing out of you are for others.

The dictionary says a *witness* is "evidence" or "confirmation." This power of the Holy Spirit living in you can transform your life into evidence for the world that Jesus has been raised from the dead and is alive today. Jesus said, "But ye shall receive power, after that the Holy Ghost is come upon you: and ye shall be witnesses unto me..." (Acts 1:8).

The traditions and doctrines of men have robbed many believers of this power to be a witness, with evidence that Jesus has been raised from the dead. The world is not only supposed to hear words but see proof that Jesus is alive today. As new converts, we should be taught to receive the Baptism in the Holy Spirit—the enduement of power to reveal Jesus to lost humanity.

Many believe that the Holy Spirit is automatically received at the time of salvation, and that's all there is. It is certainly true that if you are born again, the Holy Spirit has come to live in you and endeavors to work in your life. I had been born again and the Holy Spirit lived inside me, but the power Jesus spoke of was not evident in my life until after I received the Baptism in the Holy Spirit. I wanted to do right, follow God and be a strong Christian, but outwardly, I didn't change much until after I received the Baptism in the Holy Spirit and began to speak with other tongues. The combination of the power of God on me and The WORD of God in my heart began to change weakness to victory. As I learned truth from God's WORD and acted on it, the Spirit of God upon me enabled me to overcome in my own life and to help others overcome.

Learn to continually pray this prayer for yourself:

> For this cause I bow my knees unto the Father of our
> LORD Jesus Christ, of whom the whole family in
> heaven and earth is named, that he would grant [me],

according to the riches of his glory, to be strengthened
with might by his Spirit in [my] inner man; that Christ
may dwell in [my] heart by faith; that [I], being rooted
and grounded in love, may be able to comprehend with
all saints what is the breadth, and length, and depth, and
height; and to know the love of Christ, which passeth
knowledge, that [I] might be filled with all the fulness
of God. Now unto him that is able to do exceeding
abundantly above all that [I] ask or think, according to
the power that worketh in [me], unto him be glory in
the church by Christ Jesus throughout all ages, world
without end. Amen (Ephesians 3:14-21).

According to the power that works in us! His unlimited ability to
work in your life is according to the power working in you. God designed
that His Spirit abide continually *inside* your spirit and come *on* you in
power to carry out His work.

Frequently, in the early Church, people were born again and received
the Baptism in the Holy Spirit at the same time. In Acts 8, however, we
can see clearly that there are two different experiences. It tells us that in
Samaria, Philip preached the things concerning the kingdom of God and
the Name of Jesus. Verse 12 says they believed, and both men and women
were baptized. These people were believers.

Later, Peter and John came to pray for these same believers, that
they might receive the Holy Ghost. "(For as yet he was fallen upon none
of them: only they were baptized in the name of The LORD Jesus.)
Then laid they their hands on them, and they received the Holy Ghost"
(verses 16-17).

The term "received the Holy Ghost" is also correct in speaking
about the Baptism in the Holy Spirit because later, Paul asked the men

at Ephesus, "Have ye received the Holy Ghost since ye believed? And they said unto him, We have not so much as heard whether there be any Holy Ghost" (Acts 19:2).

> YOU RECEIVE THE BAPTISM IN THE HOLY SPIRIT BY FAITH IN THE SAME WAY YOU RECEIVE JESUS AS LORD.

These men had been baptized into John's baptism. Paul told them that John said to believe on Jesus. "When they heard this, they were baptized in the name of The LORD Jesus. And when Paul had laid his hands upon them, the Holy Ghost came on them; and they spake with tongues, and prophesied" (verses 5-6). In this instance, they were baptized in water, and then Paul laid hands on them to receive the Holy Ghost.

From these instances, we can see that the apostles laid their hands on men who were already believers to receive the Holy Spirit. These scriptures reveal that this enduement of power called the Baptism in the Holy Spirit is not the same experience as the new birth. In this instance, it came as hands were laid on them.

However, on the Day of Pentecost, at the house of Cornelius, the Spirit of God fell on those who were present, and they began to speak in other tongues. Hands were not laid on them. They received the new birth and the enduement of power simultaneously.

You receive the Baptism in the Holy Spirit by faith in the same way you receive Jesus as LORD (Galatians 3:14). Christians should be taught to believe for and receive the Baptism in the Holy Spirit. The disciples in the upper room on the Day of Pentecost had been taught about receiving the Holy Spirit by the Master (John 14-16; Luke 24:49; Acts 1).

The entrance of God's WORD gives light or understanding (Psalm 119:130). The disciples knew they were waiting for the Holy Spirit to baptize them with His power, and they were expecting it, just as Jesus told them.

We receive THE BLESSING from God by believing what we hear from Him. That is faith. For example, healing belonged to you the moment you were born into God's family, but if you never get into The WORD and see that divine health is yours, you will continue to be sick.

To walk the faith walk and be pleasing to God, His WORD must be the authority in your life—not what men or tradition says!

Learn to Depend on the Holy Spirit... He Will Guide You Into All Truth

"But as it is written, Eye hath not seen, nor ear heard, neither have entered into the heart of man, the things which God hath prepared for them that love him. But God hath revealed them unto us by his Spirit: for the Spirit searcheth all things, yea, the deep things of God" (1 Corinthians 2:9-10).

Who can know what is on the inside of a man except the man's own spirit, and who can know what is on the inside of God except the Spirit of God (verse 11)? The Spirit of God living within your spirit can reveal to you the inside of God—the heart of the Father. It is difficult to grasp that the Holy Spirit, who knows all the deep things of God, desires to come live in you in order to teach you the profound and unsearchable wisdom of God. Yet, it is true.

No man knows the things of God because they are spiritually discerned (verse 14). "But God hath revealed them unto us by His Spirit" (verse 10). These deep things of God can enter into the heart of man only by the Spirit of God.

God's WORD must be revealed to you by His Spirit before you can walk in it. Your spirit alone cannot comprehend or see into these deep things of God, but Jesus said that the Holy Spirit would teach you all things (John 14:26). He told the disciples, "I have yet many things to say unto you, but ye cannot bear them now. Howbeit when he, the Spirit of truth, is come, he will guide you into all truth: for he shall not speak of himself; but whatsoever he shall hear, that shall he speak: and he will show you things to come" (John 16:12-13).

Remember, Jesus told the disciples that the Holy Spirit was with them, but would be *in* them. Jesus told them He had many things to say to them that they could not bear or grasp at that time, but when the Spirit of truth came, He would open all things to their understanding. Without the Holy Spirit living in their spirits to reveal the truth to the disciples, even Jesus could teach them no more.

The disciples were limited in their ability to understand spiritual things.

He was telling them that there would be no limit to spiritual knowledge when the Holy Spirit came. He said the Holy Spirit would show them all things that the Father has—even things to come.

Now, can you see the limitless knowledge and understanding that is available to Spirit-filled believers? The Holy Spirit has been given to teach you how to be successful in this life. In the light of these truths from The WORD of God, it is unthinkable for a man to refuse God's offer of His Spirit!

I WILL SEND HIM UNTO YOU

"Nevertheless I tell you the truth; It is expedient for you that I go away: for if I go not away, the Comforter will not come unto you; but if I depart, I will send him unto you" (John 16:7). Jesus said, "I will send him unto you." Jesus has personally sent the Holy Spirit to you. He arrived in the fullness of His ministry on the Day of Pentecost and is still here.

"And, behold, I send the promise of my Father upon you: but tarry ye in the city of Jerusalem, until ye be endued with power from on high" (Luke 24:49). Jesus told His disciples to wait until they were furnished with power. When you made Jesus LORD, you became His disciple, and you should not do another thing until *you* are endued with the same power that was in and on Him.

On the Day of Pentecost, Peter told the people, "This Jesus hath God raised up, whereof we all are witnesses. Therefore being by the right hand of God exalted, and having received of the Father the promise of the Holy Ghost, he hath shed forth this, which ye now see and hear.... For the promise is unto you, and to your children, and to all that are afar off, even as many as The LORD our God shall call" (Acts 2:32-33, 39).

This promise of receiving the Holy Spirit is to all—as it says, "even as many as The LORD...shall call." It is to you and your children. God has already given the Body of Christ the Holy Spirit. You, as a member of the Body, must individually receive what He has already given. He has been sent to endue you with His power. You don't have to be a weak Christian. His provision has already been made for you.

If there has ever been a day when believers need the power of God manifest in their lives, it is today! Don't try to get by on your own strength any longer. Set your faith to receive this enduement of power without delay.

You may receive by having hands laid on you by a believer or someone in the ministry, or you may receive in your own place of prayer, alone with God.

Study the following scriptures about receiving the Holy Spirit so you will believe and act in line with God's WORD.

BE FILLED WITH THE SPIRIT

The Bible simply says, "Be filled with the Spirit" (Ephesians 5:18). You know the Bible is God speaking to you, and The WORD of God is the will of God. Then, in light of this scripture, *it is God's will for you to receive the Baptism in the Holy Spirit!*

> And I say unto you, Ask, and it shall be given you; seek,
> and ye shall find; knock, and it shall be opened unto you.
> For every one that asketh receiveth; and he that seeketh
> findeth; and to him that knocketh it shall be opened. If a

son shall ask bread of any of you that is a father, will he give him a stone? or if he ask a fish, will he for fish give him a serpent? or if he shall ask an egg, will he offer him a scorpion? If ye then, being evil, know how to give good gifts unto your children:

THE HOLY SPIRIT COMES TO OUR AID TO HELP US IN PRAYER WHEN WE DON'T KNOW HOW TO PRAY.

how much more shall your heavenly Father give the Holy Spirit to them that ask him? (Luke 11:9-13).

First, we see that as a son, you are to ask the Father for the Holy Spirit. Even though He has already been given to the Church, you are asking and inviting Him to come on *you* and endue *you* with power. So ask Him to baptize you in the Holy Spirit.

We are told that if we ask, we shall receive. The WORD assures you that you will receive the good gift—the Holy Spirit—not a counterfeit. Therefore, ask expectantly and without fear, knowing that your Father gives only good gifts to His children:

> And they were all filled with the Holy Ghost, and began to speak with other tongues, as the Spirit gave them utterance (Acts 2:4).

> While Peter yet spake these words, the Holy Ghost fell on all them which heard The WORD. And they of the circumcision which believed were astonished, as many as came with Peter, because that on the Gentiles also was poured out the gift of the Holy Ghost. For

> they heard them speak with tongues, and magnify God
> (Acts 10:44-46).

> And when Paul had laid his hands upon them, the Holy
> Ghost came on them; and they spake with tongues, and
> prophesied (Acts 19:6).

Notice, in the accounts of believers receiving the Holy Spirit, *they* began to speak with other tongues. Nowhere in the New Testament does it say the Holy Spirit does the speaking. The believer speaks as the Holy Spirit gives him utterance.

You supply the sounds as the Holy Spirit supplies the words. These words will be unknown to you. The Scripture teaches us that, in the spirit, we are speaking mysteries to God. "For he that speaketh in an unknown tongue speaketh not unto men, but unto God: for no man understandeth him; howbeit in the spirit he speaketh mysteries" (1 Corinthians 14:2). You are not speaking to man but to God.

One translation says we speak divine secrets. You can pray beyond your natural knowledge when you pray in other tongues.

> So too the [Holy] Spirit comes to our aid and bears us up
> in our weakness; for we do not know what prayer to offer
> nor how to offer it worthily as we ought, but the Spirit
> Himself goes to meet our supplication and pleads in our
> behalf with unspeakable yearnings and groanings too deep
> for utterance. And He Who searches the hearts of men
> knows what is in the mind of the [Holy] Spirit [what His
> intent is], because the Spirit intercedes and pleads [before
> God] in behalf of the saints according to and in harmony
> with God's will (Romans 8:26-27, *The Amplified Bible*).

The Holy Spirit comes to our aid to help us in prayer when we don't know how to pray as we ought and gives us utterance in other tongues, praying the perfect will of God. We need this help because so much of the time we know so little. Often, we may only see a symptom of a much deeper problem, but the Holy Spirit goes right to the root of it and prays the perfect will of God for us.

Look at Jude 20, *The Amplified Bible:* "But you, beloved, build yourselves up [founded] on your most holy faith [make progress, rise like an edifice higher and higher], praying in the Holy Spirit." Praying in tongues *edifies* you. This means praying in tongues builds you up or charges your spirit as we would charge a battery.

I am so grateful to be able to pray in the spirit by the Holy Spirit. This will be a great blessing to you. After you receive your prayer language, pray in the spirit every day. It helps your spirit to become strong and keep rule over your life.

First Corinthians 14:14 says, "For if I pray in an unknown tongue, my spirit prayeth, but my understanding is unfruitful." *The Amplified Bible* says, "My spirit [by the Holy Spirit within me] prays." The Holy Spirit gives your spirit the prayer or praise. Your voice gives sound to this spiritual language.

The Amplified Bible says that Cornelius and his household spoke in unknown languages and extolled and magnified God (Acts 10:46). To *extol* means "to praise enthusiastically."

When you receive the indwelling of the Holy Spirit, your spirit will immediately have a desire to express itself in praise to God. How could you help but pour forth praise after having the Holy Spirit, who proceeds directly from the Father God, come upon you in power? Your well begins to overflow and rivers are the result! (See John 4:14, 7:37-39.)

There may be no unusual feeling physically. Spiritual blessings are received by faith—not by sight or by feeling. Your lips may flutter and your tongue feel thick, or you may hear the supernatural words forming down inside your being. Or, none of these things may be evident.

The lips and tongue are the organs we use to form words. Your physical instruments of speech—lips, tongue, vocal cords—must cooperate with your spirit in order to give sound to prayer or praise that the Holy Spirit has given. Immediately, on receiving the Baptism in the Holy Spirit, spiritual language is ready for you to speak.

Remember, you have nothing to fear. God has already said you would receive the real thing. Isaiah 57:19 tells us that *God* creates the fruit of the lips. Do not be concerned with how it sounds to you. God will perfect your praise. Matthew 21:16 says, "Out of the mouth of babes and sucklings thou hast perfected praise."

Jesus said that the believer *would* speak with new tongues. "And these signs shall follow them that believe...they shall speak with new tongues" (Mark 16:17). You are a believer.

When you pray in tongues, you are praying in the spirit. Just as your native language, such as English, is the voice of your mind, praying in tongues is the voice of your spirit. Therefore, after you ask, speak no more in your native language. You cannot speak two languages at once.

Expect the Holy Spirit to come upon you, just as He came upon the believers on the Day of Pentecost, at Samaria, at Cornelius' home and at Ephesus, and you will begin to speak in other tongues as the Spirit gives you the words.

Ask and Receive!

LORD Jesus, I come to You in faith to receive the Baptism in the Holy Spirit. I ask You to fill me to overflowing with the Holy Spirit—the same enduement of power that happened on the Day of Pentecost. Cause rivers of living water to flow out of me as I give utterance to my spiritual language. I receive now in Your Name. (Now begin to speak in tongues in praise and adoration as the Spirit gives you the words.)

RELY ON YOUR COMFORTER

Jesus called the Holy Spirit the Comforter (John 14:16). *Comforter* means "counselor, helper, intercessor, advocate, strengthener, standby." Learn to rely on the Holy Spirit in all these areas of His ministry. He is the Great Enabler! Jesus said the Holy Spirit is given to teach you, not just some things, but *all* truth.

"Ye are of God, little children, and have overcome them: because greater is he that is in you, than he that is in the world" (1 John 4:4). Meditate on this verse and confess it with your lips until your spirit sings with the reality that *greater is He that is in me than he that is in the world.*

There is One on the inside to guide you who knows everything from beginning to end. Rely on His guidance and direction in every decision. Expect His power to aid you in every crisis, as well as in everyday life. He is more powerful than the enemy. Satan is no match for Him.

This great One has been instructed to lead you into all the truth (John 16:13). He *will* lead, so you be quick to follow. He will not only tell you what to do, but will help you to do it. He will empower you.

The Spirit who created the universe now dwells in you. Allow your mind to grasp what your spirit is telling you. This great One lives in you!

"But ye shall receive power, after that the Holy Ghost is come upon you..." (Acts 1:8). Something wonderful has happened to you, today. *Power! Power! Power!* You have been endued with God's power and ability! "And ye shall be witnesses unto me...." Dare to believe for this truth and power to be displayed in your life, and you will be a witness to men that Jesus is alive!

SCRIPTURE:

Nevertheless, I tell you the truth; It is expedient for you that I go away: for if I go not away, the Comforter will not come unto you; but if I depart, I will send him unto you.... I have yet many things to say unto you, but ye cannot bear them now. Howbeit when he, the Spirit of truth, is come, he will guide you into all truth: for he shall not speak of himself; but whatsoever he shall hear, that shall he speak: and he will show you things to come. He shall glorify me: for he shall receive of mine, and shall show it unto you. All things that the Father hath are mine: therefore said I, that he shall take of mine, and shall show it unto you (John 16:7, 12-15).

POINTS TO REMEMBER:

1. Jesus came to make it possible for man to receive the nature of God—eternal life (John 10:10).

2. The Bible is God speaking to you and The WORD of God is the will of God. Then in light of Ephesians 5:18, *it is God's will for you to receive the Baptism in the Holy Spirit!*

3. There is One on the inside to guide you who knows everything from beginning to end. Rely on His guidance and direction in every decision. Expect His power to aid you in every crisis, as well as in everyday life.

CONFESSION:

I am a new creature in Christ. I believe I receive the mighty Baptism in the Holy Spirit with the evidence of speaking in tongues as the Holy Spirit gives me the utterance (Acts 2:4). I am filled to overflowing with the Holy Spirit. Rivers of living water flow out of me as I give utterance to my spiritual language.

As I allow the Holy Spirit to live big in me, the fruit of joy and peace operate in my life. The LORD guides me into all truth. He prays the perfect will of God through me as I pray in other tongues by the power of the Holy Spirit. I believe I receive God's *dunamis* power—His ability and might—enabling me to walk in overcoming power to fulfill the plan of God for my life and to accomplish God's work in the earth.

CHAPTER THREE

God's Will Is His WORD

G od does not will one thing and say another. It would be dishonest and unjust for Him to not reveal His will to you and then hold you responsible for walking uprightly before Him.

Paul knew how vital it was for believers to know God's will. His Spirit-directed prayer for the Church in Colossians 1:9 was that they would be *filled* with the knowledge of God's will.

God's WORD is His will. It is supernatural and alive. The Holy Spirit is sent to reveal this supernatural WORD to you. He makes the instructions of the Father a reality. Read the Bible with the knowledge that God had it written for your benefit—not for His. He is already quite successful.

The WORD is God speaking to you, teaching you how to live an abundant and successful life.

Jesus said, "If ye abide in me,

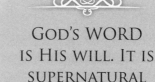

GOD'S WORD
IS HIS WILL. IT IS
SUPERNATURAL
AND ALIVE.

and my words abide in you, ye shall ask what ye will, and it shall be done unto you" (John 15:7).

God's WORD in you is the key to answered prayer.

Your Father wants you to be victorious in this life and to enjoy all the rights and privileges Jesus purchased for you. He desires that you keep His WORD because it will keep you whole—spirit, soul and body.

The world should see a Christian as The WORD sees him: a man able to control his circumstances with every physical, mental and spiritual need met.

The Bible tells you who you are and what you can do in Christ. As a born-again believer, you are *in* Christ. You are a member of the Body of Christ. "And we know that the Son of God is come, and hath given us an understanding, that we may know him that is true, and we are in him that is true, even in his Son Jesus Christ. This is the true God, and eternal life" (1 John 5:20).

Every time The WORD says "in Christ," "in whom," "in Him," *it means you!* You are in Him. As you come to these scriptures, underline each one and receive by faith what the Bible says you are. These scriptures are especially found in Paul's letters to the churches because Jesus gave Paul the revelation of the authority and redemption of the Church (Galatians 1:11-12).

As you study The WORD, underline key scriptures so you can readily find them. Don't carry a Bible in which you cannot write.

The Bible is not a book to be admired and given a place of honor on the bookshelf. It is your reference book for living. Your very life depends on what you find in it. It is the "how to" of everyday life. Keep it with you and most importantly, keep it in your heart. (Proverbs 4:20-23 tells you how.)

The Bible is God's wisdom made available to man and written in man's words. Read it positively, not as a set of rules, but as the open door to freedom. "And ye shall know the truth, and the truth shall make you free" (John 8:32).

The truth makes you free! It does not put you in bondage.

GOD'S FORMULA FOR SUCCESS

"This Book of the Law shall not depart out of your mouth, but you shall meditate on it day and night, that you may observe and do according to all that is written in it. For then you shall make your way prosperous, and then you shall deal wisely and have good success" (Joshua 1:8, *The Amplified Bible*).

God's success formula begins with keeping His WORD in your mouth. *Talk God's WORD.*

God gave Israel these instructions: "And these WORDS, which I command thee this day, shall be in thine heart: And thou shalt teach them diligently unto thy children, and shalt talk of them when thou sittest in thine house, and when thou walkest by the way, and when thou liest down, and when thou risest up" (Deuteronomy 6:6-7).

God told Israel to talk His WORD when they sat down, when they walked, when they lay down and when they rose up. That's all the time!

How could that be possible? Jesus said, "Out of the abundance of the heart the mouth speaketh" (Matthew 12:34). The words you put inside yourself are the words that come out. What words do you see and listen to most of the time—television, radio, different websites, social media, novels or God's WORD?

Listen to yourself talk, and you will know what is in you in abundance. If you are talking doubt, fear and sickness, that's what is in you in abundance. Your source of information must be changed!

The stream of things in this world is negative. Unless you take action against the world order with The WORD of God, your mouth will speak from experience, circumstance and tradition.

Jesus said, "For verily I say unto you, That whosoever shall say unto this mountain, Be thou removed, and be thou cast into the sea; and shall not doubt in his heart, but shall believe that those things which he saith shall come to pass; he shall have whatsoever he saith" (Mark 11:23).

You receive in this life just what you say with your mouth. The WORD in your mouth is your faith speaking.

The words you speak are what you believe.

Your words can be for you or against you. They bring you health or sickness, abundance or lack, victory or defeat. Solomon, the wisest and richest man in the Old Testament, said you are snared by the words of your mouth. You are set free or brought into bondage by your words.

Remember, Jesus said in Matthew 12:34, "For out of the abundance of the heart the mouth speaketh"? The mouth speaks according to what you put in your heart. Jesus continued in verse 35: "A good man out of the good treasure of the heart bringeth forth good things." Put God's WORD in your heart and you will speak it with your mouth. God's WORD in your mouth will cause good things to happen in your life.

MEDITATE ON GOD'S WORD

You put God's WORD in your heart by meditating on it. You don't change the way you believe in your heart by just *wanting* to change it. *You can only change how you believe by The WORD of God.*

"So then faith cometh by hearing, and hearing by The WORD of God" (Romans 10:17). The only way faith comes into the heart is by hearing The WORD, and the only way faith can be developed is through The WORD. There is no shortcut.

Meditation in The WORD is a necessity in God's success formula.

Keep His WORD before you and meditate—dwell on The WORD in your thought life—day and night. Meditation is more than just reading. It is *fixing your mind* on The WORD so that you do all that is written in it. You will receive revelation and insight that you could never gain by hearing only.

By meditating in The WORD, you are applying it to yourself personally and allowing the Holy Spirit to make it a reality in your heart.

> MENTAL ASSENT
> DOES NOT ACT BY
> FAITH IN THE WORD
> BUT ON WHAT IT SEES
> AND FEELS.

You are carefully pondering how it applies to your life and dwelling on how it changes your situation. Or, perhaps you will simply receive the quiet revelation of, *That means me!* You are placing yourself in agreement with what God says about you and seeing yourself as He sees you!

As long as God's WORD is just a book to you—even a holy book—you will not act on it. Until it becomes God dealing with you, it will not be active and powerful in your life.

It is through meditation that the integrity of God's WORD becomes a reality to you. As the truth is revealed in your spirit, you will begin to do all that is written in it. Acting on God's WORD is the result of keeping His WORDS in your mouth and meditating on them. It is only acting on God's WORD that guarantees success.

One of the greatest enemies of faith is mental assent. It agrees that God's WORD is true but does not act on it and therefore enjoys no results. Mental assent says, "I believe the Bible is true from Genesis to Revelation." But when it is time to apply that Word *personally,* it says, "I know the Bible says that by His stripes I am healed, but I feel sick, so I must be sick."

Mental assent does not act by faith in The WORD but on what it sees and feels. People who just agree that The WORD is true, do not walk by faith, but by sight.

Beware of the trap of mental assent. It is subtle because it sounds good. A great deal of the time mental assent can be tagged by the words *but* and *if*—two little words that will rob you of your confession of faith. Put them out of your vocabulary, and replace them with The WORD of God.

ACTING ON THE WORD

Jesus gives us an example of two men and the way they responded after hearing The WORD. The wise man acted on The WORD, and the foolish man gave mental assent to The WORD. You can be either man:

> Therefore whosoever heareth these sayings of mine, and
> doeth them, I will liken him unto a wise man, which
> built his house upon a rock: And the rain descended,
> and the floods came, and the winds blew, and beat upon
> that house; and it fell not: for it was founded upon a
> rock. And every one that heareth these sayings of mine,
> and doeth them not, shall be likened unto a foolish
> man, which built his house upon the sand: And the rain
> descended, and the floods came, and the winds blew, and
> beat upon that house; and it fell: and great was the fall of
> it (Matthew 7:24-27).

Knowing what The WORD says is not enough. *You must act on that knowledge to get results.* Both men heard The WORD, and both houses experienced the storm, but the results were different!

Acting on The WORD put a foundation under the wise man's house that could not be moved, and his house suffered no loss.

Hearing The WORD but not doing it left the foolish man's house without a foundation when the floods came. His house may have been easier to build, but it had no power to stand.

Because meditation in God's WORD makes it a reality to you, it shuts the door to mental assent and opens the door wide to doing God's WORD. It gets your thoughts and actions in line with God's will for you.

As truths are revealed to you in The WORD, apply them to your circumstances and do them. Be the wise man who acts on The WORD.

When the adversities of life come against your house, it will stand because the foundation of acting on God's WORD will *make it stand*.

Learn to act on The WORD of God just as you would the word of your doctor, lawyer or best friend. For example, in the area of healing, meditate on this scripture: "Surely He has borne our griefs (sicknesses, weaknesses, and distresses) and carried our sorrows and pains...and with the stripes [that wounded] Him we are healed and made whole" (Isaiah 53:4-5, *The Amplified Bible*). Apply this scripture to yourself by fixing your mind on Jesus carrying your sickness or pain in His own body. Dwell on the fact that He took this for you, and by His stripes *you were healed.*

Faith will begin to rise within you to grasp hold of the truth that Jesus made you free from sickness and pain just as surely as He made you free from sin.

As you apply these scriptures to your body and meditate on God's WORD that "...by His stripes you were healed," healing will become a reality in your heart. (See also 1 Peter 2:24.) Then, as you act on that WORD, healing will take place in your body, and it will prosper and begin to enjoy good success.

Revelation of The WORD in your mind and spirit (heart) opens the door for physical healing. The physical world follows after the spiritual. "Beloved, I wish above all things that thou mayest prosper and be in health, even as thy soul prospereth" (3 John 2). "He sent His WORD, and healed them, and delivered them from their destructions" (Psalm 107:20).

Use this example of God's formula for success to obtain His will for you in every area of life.

God's answer to every problem common to man is found in His WORD. For every evil Satan can throw at mankind, our Father has provided The WORD to overcome it. Prosperity and good success are yours through God's WORD. "If ye abide in me, and my words abide in you, ye shall ask what ye will, and it shall be done unto you" (John 15:7).

SUMMARY

To put this formula into action, first find out what God says in His WORD about the need in your life. Then, keep that scripture in your mouth. Talk God's WORD.

Next, meditate—or apply—what God has said, to your situation. As you meditate, *see your need met by God's solution.* And, most importantly, *do* God's WORD. Fearlessly act on what you see in The WORD, knowing that no word from God is without power.

When you do these things, good success is inevitable. You are dealing wisely because you are utilizing God's wisdom. God says by doing these things, you make your way prosperous. His formula does not fail!

Meditating in God's WORD causes you to be able to do God's WORD. Doing God's WORD causes you to make your way prosperous. Then, you will deal wisely and have good success.

You will rejoice in The LORD as your life becomes that of the man described in Psalm 1:

> BLESSED is the man that walketh not in the counsel of the ungodly, nor standeth in the way of sinners, nor sitteth in the seat of the scornful. But his delight is in the law of The LORD; and in his law doth he meditate day and night. And he shall be like a tree planted by the rivers of water, that bringeth forth his fruit in his season; his leaf also shall not wither; and whatsoever he doeth shall prosper. The ungodly are not so: but are like the chaff which the wind driveth away. Therefore the ungodly shall not stand in the judgment, nor sinners in the congregation of the righteous. For The LORD knoweth the way of the righteous: but the way of the ungodly shall perish.

When your delight is in The LORD and you meditate in His WORD day and night, you will not walk after the counsel of men but of God, delighting and meditating in His WORD—becoming like a tree planted by the water: You will not be moved, and you will bring forth fruit. Whatever you do will prosper because you walk in the counsel of Almighty God. The LORD will be ever aware of your well-being for He knows the way of the righteous.

THE HIGHER LIFE

"For my thoughts are not your thoughts, neither are your ways my ways, saith The LORD. For as the heavens are higher than the earth, so are my ways higher than your ways, and my thoughts than your thoughts" (Isaiah 55:8-9).

As you meditate, act on God's WORD and walk in the counsel of God, you begin to conform to your Father's way of life. This is the process the Apostle Paul speaks of as "the renewing of your mind:" He says in Romans 12:2: "And be not conformed to this world: but be ye transformed by the renewing of your mind, that ye may prove what is that good, and acceptable, and perfect, will of God."

Your mind has been trained for years to respect and conform to the wisdom of this world, governed by the world's standards and approval. James says this wisdom does not come from above but is earthly, sensual and devilish (James 3:15). It is the wisdom of selfishness. It makes no provision for the powerful, unseen realm of the spirit.

The WORD simply says, "Be not conformed to this world."

To break conformity with the world, your mind must be renewed to think in line with God's WORD. In every area of life, begin to lay aside tradition and the standards of the world when they oppose God's WORD.

"Casting down imaginations, and every high thing that exalteth itself against the knowledge of God, and bringing into captivity every thought to the obedience of Christ" (2 Corinthians 10:5).

Reject the imaginations and thoughts that would place themselves in authority above God's WORD. Every thought should be governed by what The WORD says. You will begin to unconsciously judge everything you hear by, "What does The WORD say about that?"

As you continue to feed on The WORD of God, your mind becomes like a carefully programmed computer. When information comes into it contrary to what The WORD says, your mind deliberately casts it out.

You are making God's ways your ways and His thoughts your thoughts. His ways are as much higher than man's ways as the heavens are higher than the earth. As you renew your mind through His WORD, you become transformed to His way. You begin to know His will for your life and walk in it.

The renewing of your mind begins on a faith basis. Determine that you are going to believe God's WORD, regardless of what tradition or the world's wisdom says. Make your commitment, by faith, to let The WORD be your supreme authority. This commitment to The WORD is the open door to God's higher way of life.

Jesus said, "Whoever finds his [lower] life will lose [the higher life], and whoever loses his [lower] life on My account will find it [the higher life]" (Matthew 10:39, *The Amplified Bible*).

The lower life Jesus is speaking of is lived in the world's wisdom—or the realm of the five senses. It is governed by seeing, hearing, feeling, tasting or smelling and is limited to the natural world.

The higher life is a life in tune with God—transformed by His WORD. It is walking in the spirit and counsel of the Most High and centers on the great God of the universe. It has no limit.

If men could see the greatness and freedom of this higher life in God's wisdom, they would not hesitate to embrace it. It is so much greater and more powerful than the sense-ruled life that they would make it their greatest quest.

But, you cannot experience the higher life first and *then* take it by faith. You cannot hold on to the lower life—being ruled by your senses—and try the life in the spirit. You have to take God's WORD for it, letting go of the lower life by faith in God's WORD, *before* you can see into the higher life.

You enter into the higher life by faith—faith in what God says.

GIVE THE WORD FIRST PLACE

"[For skillful and godly Wisdom is the principal thing].... Prize Wisdom highly and exalt her, and she will exalt and promote you; she will bring you to honor when you embrace her" (Proverbs 4:7-8, *The Amplified Bible*).

Wisdom is the principal thing! The dictionary says *principal* means "first in importance." God's WORD is His wisdom. Giving The WORD first place in your life is the only way His wisdom can obtain its rightful position. The Bible is God's wisdom written for man. He has sent His WORD to you so you can operate in His wisdom on the earth.

You are exalting the wisdom of God when you make His WORD the authority in your life. Just hearing and acquiring knowledge of God's WORD is not enough to bring results. Wisdom is the ability to use knowledge. *Acting on this knowledge will cause God's WORD to be fulfilled in your life.* You are bringing your life into obedience to His wisdom.

Walking in God's wisdom is acting on His WORD, which then puts it into operation on your behalf. As you see it produce in your life, you will begin to prize and treasure His wisdom above all things that can be desired (Proverbs 3:15).

Put The WORD first in your life and exalt it, and it will exalt and promote you. The WORD of God in the heart and mouth of even the most unassuming will exalt them. "Prize Wisdom highly and exalt her, and she will exalt and promote you; she will bring you to honor when you embrace her" (Proverbs 4:8, *The Amplified Bible*).

You give The WORD first place in your life in two ways:

1. Arrange your schedule around The WORD, instead of trying to make The WORD fit into your busy life.

2. Make what God says the authority in your life: Believe what God says to you in The WORD, and act on it.

As you mentally plan each day, automatically set aside time to study The WORD first.

I heard a man of God say that God had spoken to him and told him that if he would read the Gospels and the book of Acts three times in 30 days, he would have a greater revelation of Jesus.

When I heard this, I was impressed that The LORD wanted me to do the same thing. I certainly desired a greater revelation of Jesus, but it could not have come at a more inopportune time.

We had just left the business world and moved to Tulsa, Oklahoma, so Kenneth could enroll at Oral Roberts University. (We had come to Tulsa by faith. For the first time in our lives, we were in the will of God. How great it was to be in the right place at the right time for a change!)

Everything at our house was still upside down. We had not even finished unpacking. The children were at a very demanding age—they would not wait 30 minutes, much less 30 days! Kellie was 3 years old and John was 9 months old. *Where would I get the time?*

All these obstacles loomed before me, but God said do it.

I told Kenneth I might not have time to cook or to iron his shirts, but whatever it took, I was going to read the Gospels and Acts three times in 30 days. He readily agreed that I should do it.

There were so many things I had planned to do, it was hard for me to put the work aside. But, I decided that I could stand anything for 30 days. I determined to postpone the other things until I had finished my assignment.

I figured out how many pages I would read each day in my *Amplified*

Bible so I wouldn't get behind. It came to four hours or more daily—most of which had to be read while the children were asleep.

I set aside three times each day to read. I got up at 5:30 a.m. and read until everyone got up. Then when the children took their naps in the afternoon, I read again as long as I could. At night I would go to bed and finish whatever I lacked from that day's reading.

Regardless of what happened or what needed to be done, I put reading God's WORD first.

I thought the other things would just have to wait until the next month, but God had a pleasant surprise for me!

When I committed myself to Him by putting His WORD first place in my life, I opened the door for God to commit Himself to me.

The very first day I started, I sat down at 3 o'clock in the afternoon with my day's work done, and I had already spent hours in The WORD!

At the end of the first week, I had accomplished putting The WORD before anything else. I had also painted and antiqued four pieces of furniture from start to finish, done the ironing (accumulated for weeks), and had my house in order. I was amazed! I could never have done all of that under normal conditions.

We knew very little then about how to live by faith. I did not know that The WORD makes your way prosperous and causes good success, or that if you put God's wisdom first, it will exalt and promote you. But, I experienced a miracle of God just the same. By faith, I had put His WORD first.

You will never get into The WORD if you wait until you have time. Satan will see to it that you never have time. He is vehemently against your feeding on God's WORD. *He knows it is The WORD that makes you free from his dominion!* Give The WORD first place in your schedule, and everything else will come into agreement with God's will for your life. Jesus said, "But seek ye first the kingdom of God, and his righteousness; and all these things shall be added unto you" (Matthew 6:33).

This is the result of exalting The WORD before everything else. You now know to expect a miracle in your time before you start. Whether you are a housewife, a mechanic or a businessman—you need to commit yourself to God's WORD.

EXALT THE WORD OF GOD IN YOUR LIFE, AND IT WILL EXALT AND PROMOTE YOU.

Learn to set aside less important things to find out what God is saying to you in His WORD. Exalt The WORD in your life, and The WORD will exalt and promote you.

Putting The WORD first is something you will have to do continually. When you get behind and find yourself bogged down in the affairs of life, without fail, you can look back over the previous few days and realize that your time in The WORD was spent for something else.

Guard your time in The WORD. Satan will try to steal it from you. He will use everything from television to church activities—things that look good—to lure you away from God's wisdom.

CHOOSE THE GOOD PORTION

Now it came to pass, as they went, that he entered into a certain village: and a certain woman named Martha received him into her house. And she had a sister called Mary, which also sat at Jesus' feet, and heard His WORD. But Martha was cumbered about much serving, and came to him, and said, LORD, dost thou not care that my sister hath left me to serve alone? bid her therefore that she help me. And Jesus answered and said unto her, Martha, Martha, thou art careful and troubled about many things: But one thing is needful: and Mary hath chosen that good part, which shall not be taken away from her (Luke 10:38-42).

Martha thought she had to prepare a big dinner for the Master. I am sure it seemed like the only proper thing for her to do. After all, Jesus and His crusade team were staying in her home!

I can just see Martha stirring around the kitchen banging pots and pans and feeling sorry for herself. She wanted Jesus to rebuke Mary, but instead, the Master was pleased that Mary had put His WORD first.

Jesus told Martha that she was anxious and troubled about many things. She could have been at the Master's feet had she chosen that one necessary thing—The WORD.

Jesus had fed thousands with a few loaves and fishes. He could have supernaturally prepared a banquet for all those present that day!

Mary sat at Jesus' feet and heard The WORD—The WORD that could never be taken away from her. Even after The LORD Jesus went to sit at the Father's right hand, Mary still had His WORD alive in her heart.

You have the same choice today. There are still many things to be anxious and troubled about and more things to do than time to do them. But, there is still only one thing that is needful—The WORD of God.

You may look at Martha and think, *What an opportunity she wasted! I would never do that!* But, every time you allow things to swallow up *your* time in The WORD, you are passing up the opportunity to sit at the Master's feet! Jesus makes Himself real to you as you read and meditate in His WORD.

JESUS REVEALS HIMSELF THROUGH THE WORD

> He that hath my commandments, and keepeth them, he
> it is that loveth me: and he that loveth me shall be loved
> of my Father, and I will love him, and will manifest my-
> self to him. Judas saith unto him, not Iscariot, LORD,
> how is it that thou wilt manifest thyself unto us, and

not unto the world? Jesus answered and said unto him,
If a man love me, he will keep my words: and my Father
will love him, and we will come unto him, and make our
abode with him. He that loveth me not keepeth not my
sayings: and The WORD which ye hear is not mine, but
the Father's which sent me (John 14:21-24).

Jesus taught His disciples that the man who hears His WORD and
acts on it is the man who loves Him. The man who loves Jesus will also be
loved by the Father.

Jesus promised to manifest Himself—or make Himself real—to the
man who keeps His commandments. Judas wanted to know how Jesus
would make Himself real to His disciples and not to the world. The
LORD answered, "If a man love me, he will keep my WORDS...." *Jesus
reveals Himself through His WORD.*

He added that the man who does not love Him will not keep His
sayings. By not giving The WORD place in his life, this man closes the
door to the revelation of Jesus.

If you will keep His WORD, Jesus said He will make Himself real to
you. This alone is incentive enough to keep His WORD ever before you.

Jesus and the Father will come and make their dwelling place with
the man who keeps The WORD!

The more place you give His WORD in your life, the greater will be
your revelation of the Master.

MAKE GOD'S WORD FINAL AUTHORITY

Making God's WORD final authority is believing what The WORD
says rather than believing people, Satan or circumstances.

What God says should settle the issues of life as far as you are concerned. Believe you are what God says you are. Believe you can do what
God says you can do. Know you have what God says is yours.

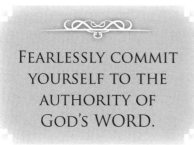

FEARLESSLY COMMIT YOURSELF TO THE AUTHORITY OF GOD'S WORD.

God is the authority in your life. Whatever He says to you in His WORD—do it. Have confidence that your Father will perform for you all that He says.

Determine in your heart that His WORD is for your advantage and that you will act on it in faith, knowing that He is the God of love. It will only become alive to you when you accept it as truth and act on it. Fearlessly commit yourself to the authority of God's WORD.

Make up your mind to walk by faith and not by sight. Be ready to act on God's WORD, even when common sense says do something else. *Common* means "ordinary." God's WORD gets you out of the ordinary and puts you into the supernatural realm of God's power! Making it final authority does not limit your life but makes all things possible to you.

The Scripture says of our God, "He is the Rock, His work is perfect, for all His ways are law and justice. A God of faithfulness without breach or deviation, just and right is He" (Deuteronomy 32:4, *The Amplified Bible*). What an assurance in a day when men's hearts are failing them because of fear!

The world's order of things is unsure and indefinite. Situations are flaunted in our faces that years ago we never dreamed possible—violence, lawlessness, narcotics, nudity and immorality. The world condemns a thing today and condones it tomorrow.

Young people want authority. They have rebelled against the world's double standard. "Because this is the way we've always done it," means nothing to them. They don't care what has always been done. They just want something to depend on that will relieve the pressures of life.

God says, "I am The LORD, I change not..." (Malachi 3:6). In the authority of God's WORD, there is certainty. Young people are flocking to hear the authority of The WORD. They quickly realize that God has no double standard. The WORD does not say one thing today and something else tomorrow. "Jesus Christ the same yesterday, and to day, and for ever," is a message they are ready to hear (Hebrews 13:8).

For the first time in their lives, many are finding that the Rock of The WORD of God is their fail-safe in this hour. The WORD does not compromise before them and neither do the Christians who have made God's WORD final authority.

They refuse the social religion they have been handed in the Name of The LORD, and who can blame them? It is full of holes and doesn't work when you need it. For the most part, it has been tradition and more talk, with little action and few results. But, what God says changes things. The WORD works!

God's WORD Is His Covenant

"He hath remembered his covenant for ever, The WORD which he commanded to a thousand generations" (Psalm 105:8). God's WORD is His covenant. His WORD is forever settled in heaven. When we speak of God's WORD, we are not speaking of a book. This Book is The WORD of God written down. It is His bond—His integrity.

In studying the old and new covenants, you will readily see that God does not hesitate to use His supernatural power to intervene in the lives of men who act on His WORD—men who put their trust in their covenant with God Almighty.

Vine's Expository Dictionary of Biblical Words, by W.E. Vine, reveals a thrilling fact about the Greek word *covenant.* The *King James Version* of the New Testament translates the same Greek word *diatheke* as both "covenant" and "testament." Mr. Vine leaves little doubt that the more literal translation of this word is "covenant." [2]

Turn to the front of your Bible, and you will find written there:

---

2   *Vine's Expository Dictionary of Biblical Words,* W.E. Vine, Merrill F. Unger, William White (ed.) (Nashville: Thomas Nelson Publishers, 1985) p. 135.

"Containing the Old and New Testaments." It could be accurately written "containing the Old and New Covenants."

God's covenant with you is His WORD!

Most Christians don't even realize they have a covenant with God. Ignorance of this covenant is the reason for failure in the Christian's life and in the Church in general. God said, "My people are destroyed for lack of knowledge…" (Hosea 4:6).

ABRAHAM'S COVENANT

And when Abram was ninety years old and nine, The LORD appeared to Abram, and said unto him, I am the Almighty God; walk before me, and be thou perfect. And I will make my covenant between me and thee, and will multiply thee exceedingly…. As for me, behold, my covenant is with thee, and thou shalt be a father of many nations. (Abram and Sarai had no children but God said,) Neither shall thy name any more be called Abram, but thy name shall be Abraham; for a father of many nations have I made thee…. This is my covenant, which ye shall keep, between me and you and thy seed after thee; Every man child among you shall be circumcised (Genesis 17:1-2, 4-5, 10).

A *covenant* in our language means a "contract" or an "agreement to do something specific." In a covenant, two parties are represented. Both parties commit themselves to do what the agreement says.

God's covenant with Abraham was more powerful than an agreement. This covenant was made law in the spirit world by the shedding of blood.

In a blood covenant, the two parties actually become related to each other in everything they do and have. They become one in an unbreakable agreement.

God told Abraham what He would do if Abraham kept the covenant. God said, "As for Me," and gave Abraham the terms of the covenant. He gave Abraham His WORD that He would be a God to him and his seed after him.

Speaking in faith of things that were not as though they were, The LORD told Abraham He had made him a father. It was physically impossible for Abraham and Sarah to have a child—*but God said!* What He says changes impossibilities into fact. His WORD is alive and powerful and able to accomplish or bring to pass.

God also promised Abraham and his seed all the land of Canaan for an everlasting possession. This was God's side of the agreement. God could bring to pass His part of the covenant, making a 100-year-old man a father, and He could give Abraham the Promised Land—*but God could not fulfill Abraham's part of the covenant.*

Abraham and his seed were responsible for their side of the agreement. By the shedding of his own blood in circumcision, a man entered into this covenant. Circumcision sealed the agreement with God. "And the uncircumcised man child whose flesh of his foreskin is not circumcised, that soul shall be cut off from his people; he hath broken my covenant" (Genesis 17:14).

The fulfillment of the covenant required the action of both parties. Neither God nor Abraham alone could cause this covenant to come to pass. God had to have a man who would carry out His instructions, and Abraham had to have the power of Almighty God.

Abraham believed and acted on God's WORD, not looking at his body, now "old and well stricken in age," nor the fact that it had "ceased to be with Sarah after the manner of women" (Genesis 18:11).

What brought this great miracle to pass in Abraham's life? Was it something not available to God's people today—something that has "passed away" or offered only to a special few?

Many would like to think this way, but these things are not true.

Reliance on The WORD of his God brought about the miracle in Abraham's life! "He staggered not at the promise of God through unbelief; but was strong in faith, giving glory to God; and being fully persuaded that, what he had promised, he was able also to perform" (Romans 4:20-21).

Later, God told Moses exactly what the children of Israel were to do, and Moses recorded what God said. Many people think God made these laws and statutes in order to rule over His people. To the natural mind, it seems God's laws were unnecessarily harsh, but only by obeying them could Israel live under the umbrella of God's BLESSING and be free from the curse on the world brought about because of Adam's treason in the Garden.

> And it shall come to pass, if thou shalt hearken diligently unto the voice of The LORD thy God, to observe and to do all his commandments which I command thee this day, that The LORD thy God will set thee on high above all nations of the earth: And all these blessings shall come on thee, and overtake thee, if thou shalt hearken unto the voice of The LORD thy God (Deuteronomy 28:1-2).

Just knowing what the covenant said was not enough. Israel had to diligently observe and *do* the commandments. The Israelites were living in a world dominated by the evil ruler Satan. They were powerless to deal with him.

God desired Israel to live in THE BLESSING, but Adam, by his own free will, placed himself and his descendants under Satan's rule. They were spiritually dead men and had little insight into the nature of God.

God had to give Israel laws covering every area of life so that they could, if they chose to obey, live out from under Satan's dominion. "Ye shall walk in all the ways which The LORD your God hath commanded you...that ye may prolong your days in the land which ye shall possess" (Deuteronomy 5:33).

This verse clearly shows that God gave Israel these laws for their well-being. Through obedience to God's WORD, they could possess the land and control their circumstances.

In spite of Satan's authority over the world and his host of evil spirits, God made a way, through His commandments, for His people to be BLESSED. *But they had to obey and do what He said.* If they did not keep His WORD, the curse would come on them, which included consumption, fever, inflammation, pestilence, famine, sores that would not heal, madness, blindness and every sickness—all that Satan still offers to the world today. They would be cursed in all their ways and oppressed and spoiled, evermore. Their lives would hang in doubt before them, and they would live in fear day and night, having no assurance of their life. They would live in poverty and lack and be in bondage to others (Deuteronomy 28).

However, by keeping God's covenant, they could be protected from this terrible curse and live in plenty, prospering in all that they did. Obedience would cause Israel to be kept by the power of God.

THE BLESSING of Abraham

God gave Moses the law and the commandments because of His covenant with Abraham. Deuteronomy 28:1-2 gives THE BLESSING of keeping the commandments:

> And it shall come to pass, if thou shalt hearken diligently
> unto the voice of The LORD thy God, to observe and
> to do all his commandments which I command thee this
> day, that The LORD thy God will set thee on high above
> all nations of the earth: And all these BLESSINGS shall
> come on thee, and overtake thee, if thou shalt hearken
> unto the voice of The LORD thy God.

If Israel walked in the covenant, they were BLESSED in the city and in the field. Their children were BLESSED, their livestock was BLESSED, and their ground brought forth abundant crops. They were BLESSED going in and coming out. The covenant guaranteed divine protection from their enemies: "The LORD shall cause thine enemies that rise up against thee to be smitten before thy face: they shall come out against thee one way, and flee before thee seven ways" (verse 7).

If the children of Israel walked in the covenant, their storehouses were BLESSED, and all they set their hand to do prospered. The people of the earth would see that they were called by the Name of The LORD, and would be afraid of them.

The covenant people were made plenteous in goods by the hand of The LORD, and His good treasure was open to them. They became the head and not the tail and could lend to many, but needed to borrow from none.

God put Himself under obligation to meet their every need. They were to be completely sustained by their God.

All these provisions God offered Israel—wealth, protection, health and success—are *yours through Jesus.* "And if ye be Christ's, then are ye Abraham's seed, and heirs according to the promise" (Galatians 3:29). It is an everlasting agreement. God told Abraham, "And I will establish my covenant between me and thee and thy seed after thee in their generations for an everlasting covenant, to be a God unto thee, and to thy seed after thee" (Genesis 17:7).

Every believer should know THE BLESSING and the curse of the law. You have been made free from the curse, and THE BLESSING of Abraham belongs to you in Jesus Christ. "Christ hath redeemed us from the curse of the law, being made a curse for us: for it is written, Cursed is every one that hangeth on a tree: That THE BLESSING of Abraham might come on the Gentiles through Jesus Christ; that we might receive the promise of the Spirit through faith" (Galatians 3:13-14).

You have been redeemed from the curse of the law. Deuteronomy 28:61 says that every sickness and every plague not even written in the book of the law is under the curse. You have been redeemed from *every* sickness. You have been redeemed from fear and poverty. Learn Deuteronomy 28 and you will better understand your redemption.

Your redemption from the curse is a powerful weapon in standing for healing and for the abundant life.

If, for example, you have fever in your body, put these scriptures before you and say, "Deuteronomy 28:22 says fever is under the curse of the law. I have been redeemed from the curse of the law. Christ has been made a curse for me."

James 4:7 instructs you to resist the devil, and he will flee from you. By speaking your redemption, this is exactly what you are doing. You are resisting the devil's sickness, poverty and doubt. Deuteronomy 28:66 says that part of the curse is: "And thy life shall hang in doubt before thee; and thou shalt fear day and night, and shalt have none assurance of thy life."

We have been redeemed from doubt and fear. You never have to doubt or be afraid again. You can live in doubt if you want to, but Jesus paid the price to make you free.

Act on God's WORD, and refuse the curse of the law that Satan is trying to put on you. Read Galatians 3:13 aloud, and apply God's WORD to your situation. It is your statement of faith.

Then, turn to THE BLESSING and find the verses that promise you victory in this area. Lay hold of THE BLESSING in faith. Then read aloud Galatians 3:14 that says THE BLESSING of Abraham is yours through Jesus Christ.

Hold fast to your confession of faith—the results are inevitable.

You have acted on the covenant. God's WORD is His covenant. He backs it with Himself.

All heaven is behind you when you act on God's WORD, as you would act on the word of your lawyer, doctor or most trusted friend.

As you go about your day, continue to confess THE BLESSING scriptures simply because they belong to you. Meditate and feed on all THE BLESSING of Abraham.

Believe for the manifestation of THE BLESSING in your life, and learn to live in it. It belongs to you. *You are a covenant person.*

COVENANT MEN IN ACTION

God told Abraham that He would establish this covenant with him for an everlasting covenant. When God speaks, His WORD remains alive and powerful through the ages.

Throughout the Old Testament, God's agreement with Abraham dictated His dealings with Israel. The nation of Israel would never have come into being without the covenant, nor could it have been sustained through the centuries without it.

Israel was miraculously brought out of Egypt because God remembered His covenant with Abraham (Psalm 105:42-43; Exodus 2:24). God had bound Himself to Israel, and Israel was bound to God. Because of His agreement, He brought the children of Israel out of Egypt with signs and wonders.

God parted the Red Sea, and Israel crossed on dry land. He did not allow even their feet to get muddy. "He brought them forth also with silver and gold: and there was not one feeble person among their tribes" (Psalm 105:37). The LORD went before them by day in a pillar of cloud to lead them, and by night in a pillar of fire to give light. He fed them with bread from heaven for 40 years in the wilderness and provided water in the desert. Even their shoes did not wear out.

The children of Israel were His covenant people! He was quick to use His miraculous power to meet their every need. He had given His WORD to Abraham and to his seed.

Moses interceded for the people of Israel when God said He would consume them for worshiping the golden calf. Moses said, "Remember

Abraham, Isaac, and Israel, thy servants, to whom thou swearest by thine own self, and saidest unto them, I will multiply your seed as the stars of heaven, and all this land that I have spoken of will I give unto your seed, and they shall inherit it for ever" (Exodus 32:13).

When Moses reminded God of the covenant, God "repented"—changed His mind (verse 14). Moses was a man who knew he had a covenant. He lived to the age of 120, and Deuteronomy 34:7, *New Living Translation* says "when he died...his eyesight was clear, and he was as strong as ever."

As long as Israel kept the covenant, no army could stand before them. Joshua was a mighty man in The LORD, and under his fearless leadership, the children of Israel took possession of the land of Canaan. He led Israel in many great victories because he knew God was with him. Joshua fearlessly acted in faith before the enemy, and The LORD gave them into his hand.

> Then Joshua spoke to The LORD on the day when The LORD gave the Amorites over to the Israelites, and he said in the sight of Israel, Sun, be silent and stand still at Gibeon, and you, moon, in the Valley of Ajalon! And the sun stood still, and the moon stayed, until the nation took vengeance upon their enemies.... There was no day like it before or since, when The LORD heeded the voice of a man. For The LORD fought for Israel (Joshua 10:12-14, *The Amplified Bible*).

Joshua kept God's covenant, leaving nothing undone of all that The LORD commanded Moses. He also saw to it that Israel obeyed God's commandments. Joshua took the whole land (Joshua 11:23). Praise The LORD! No enemy could stand before him because he kept God's WORD.

Other great men of faith like Samson, Solomon, Elisha, Elijah, Samuel, Noah, Joseph—are just a few of God's covenant men in action. All these great men had one thing in common: They knew their covenant with God and walked in it.

DAVID

David is another thrilling example of a man who knew his covenant rights. When asking Saul's men of war about Goliath, he demanded, "For who is this uncircumcised Philistine, that he should defy the armies of the living God?" (1 Samuel 17:26). David knew the giant was uncircumcised and had no covenant with God. David's strength was in The LORD. *He had a covenant with Almighty God.*

"David said moreover, The LORD that delivered me out of the paw of the lion, and out of the paw of the bear, he will deliver me out of the hand of this Philistine.... Then said David to the Philistine...I come to thee in the name of The LORD of hosts, the God of the armies of Israel, whom thou hast defied. This day will The LORD deliver thee into mine hand" (verses 37, 45-46).

None of Israel would meet the great Philistine. They were in fear and trembling before him. But young David knew The WORD of his God that said: "The LORD shall cause thine enemies that rise up against thee to be smitten before thy face" (Deuteronomy 28:7).

That's just what happened that day when the young shepherd boy slew the giant! The LORD delivered the great Philistine warrior into David's hand, and David took him with a sling and a stone (1 Samuel 17:50).

The LORD had told the Prophet Samuel He had provided Himself a king (1 Samuel 16:1). That king was David, whom The LORD described as a man after His own heart (Acts 13:22).

David and his mighty men could not be defeated: "Thus The LORD preserved and gave victory to David wherever he went" (1 Chronicles 18:6, *The Amplified Bible*). David said that The LORD delivered him from his strong enemy—from those who were too strong for him.

He said that *by his God* he could run through a troop and leap over a wall. The LORD girded him with strength for battle—supernatural strength (2 Samuel 22:30, 40).

One of David's mighty chiefs wielded his spear and killed 800 men in a day (2 Samuel 23:8). Another killed 300 men at one time (1 Chronicles 11:11). "And the fame of David went out into all lands; and The LORD brought the fear of him upon all nations" (1 Chronicles 14:17).

What made the power of God so available to David and his mighty men? David himself gives the answer: "For I have kept the ways of The LORD, and have not wickedly departed from my God. For all his judgments were before me: and as for his statutes, I did not depart from them" (2 Samuel 22:22-23).

When David and Israel sinned and did not heed the commandments of God, they could not stand against their enemies. David knew his strength was in The LORD. He knew God was his rock and fortress. Read the psalm of David in 2 Samuel 22 for more insight into this man who was so very strong in The LORD and in the power of His might.

Many years later, at the end of his life, among David's last words were, "Yet he hath made with me an everlasting covenant, ordered in all things, and sure" (2 Samuel 23:5). He was confident that even death could not affect his everlasting covenant with the Almighty—that God's WORD was sure and would not fail. He trusted in his covenant with Almighty God.

JESUS

"But when the fulness of the time was come, God sent forth his Son, made of a woman, made under the law" (Galatians 4:4).

Jesus was born of a woman, under the law. He ministered as a prophet under the Abrahamic covenant. (He referred to Himself as a prophet in Matthew 13:57.) He walked in all the ordinances of God, without sin.

Philippians 2:7 *(The Amplified Bible),* tells us that Jesus stripped Himself of His deity and became like men. He performed the miracles during His ministry by His covenant as an Israelite and not as the Son of God.

"For since He Whom God has sent speaks the WORDS of God... God does not give Him His Spirit sparingly or by measure, but boundless is the gift God makes of His Spirit!" (John 3:34, *The Amplified Bible).*

The Spirit operated without measure in Jesus' life because He spoke The WORDS of God.

THE BLESSING and the promises of Abraham's covenant belong to you in addition to THE BLESSING of the new covenant that Jesus endorsed with His own blood. He is the mediator of a better covenant established upon better promises (Hebrews 8:6).

When you study what men did under the old covenant, it enlarges your mind and spirit to grasp what is available to you in this better covenant, sealed with the blood of Jesus.

You are a covenant man!

THE NEW COVENANT

The Amplified Bible translation of Hebrews 8:6 tells us this new covenant is superior and more excellent than the old covenant and "rests upon more important (sublimer, higher, and nobler) promises."

In the old covenant, God established the priesthood to provide a way for the Israelites to cover or atone for sin—the breaking of the Old Covenant Law. The high priest offered a blood sacrifice each year which he took into the holy of holies to cover the sins of the people. When the high priest failed, the people had no approach to God.

By the shedding of his own blood through circumcision, a man entered into the Abrahamic covenant. Through the shedding of the blood of bulls and goats, he was cleansed from sin and kept under the protection of that covenant (Leviticus 17:11). But, the old covenant could only offer the *promise* of the new birth and eternal life. So Abraham's faith was accredited to him as righteousness (Romans 4:22).

Old covenant men did not receive the fulfillment of the redemption of their spirits until *after* Jesus paid the price for them to be reborn. He then took them out of Abraham's bosom into heaven (Psalm 68:18; Ephesians 4:8).

The sacrifices of the old covenant atoned for sin, or made possible a purifying of the flesh, and had to be made each year (Hebrews 9:13). The new covenant was necessary in order for the old covenant to be fulfilled (verse 15).

Jesus bore, once and for all, the sins of the first covenant and conquered sin for all who will accept His sacrifice and enter into the new covenant (verse 15). The blood of Christ, who offered Himself without spot to God, purges, or cleanses, the conscience or spirit (verse 14). The blood of animals atoned for, or covered, sin. The blood of Jesus remitted, or put away, sin, once and for all. Hebrews 10:12 says, "But this man, after he had offered one sacrifice for sins for ever, sat down on the right hand of God."

Natural man had lost his standing with God and had no approach to Him. But now, through Jesus—the go-between, or mediator, between God and man (Hebrews 8:6) has been given the only way back into the presence of God (Acts 4:12).

This new covenant is made between Jesus and the Father and is validated, forever, by the blood of the spotless Son. We have the assurance that this covenant will be kept perfectly. We know that neither the Father nor the Son will fail. Consequently, this covenant carries no curse with it—only BLESSING.

No man can stop or break this covenant except in his own life—if he refuses to walk in it. This covenant is not dependent on man. The new covenant will be kept perfectly, regardless of man's position. It is The WORD of God. It remains alive, full of power and offered to whosoever will.

"If we endure, we shall also reign with Him. If we deny and disown and reject Him, He will also deny and disown and reject us. If we are faithless [do not believe and are untrue to Him], He remains true (faithful to His WORD and His righteous character), for He cannot deny Himself" (2 Timothy 2:12-13, *The Amplified Bible*).

Jesus is the surety, or guarantee, of this new covenant (Hebrews 7:22). He stands behind every word of it. His words in Matthew 28:18 then take on even greater meaning, "All power is given unto me in heaven and in earth."

The shedding of His blood opened the way for every person into this better covenant. It has been provided for the world, but every person must individually accept the sacrifice of Calvary, knowing that Jesus paid the price for *him*. He then must act on that knowledge and make Jesus LORD over his life, believing in his heart that God raised Jesus from the dead (Romans 10:9).

Circumcision was the seal of the first covenant—man had to shed his own blood to get into the Abrahamic covenant. But Jesus shed *His* blood for man as an everlasting offering in this new covenant. He provided the blood sacrifice *for* you. The new birth is the seal of this better covenant (Hebrews 8:6).

The moment you made Jesus your LORD, you entered into this blood covenant relationship with God. All that the Father has, He turned over to Jesus in the new covenant (John 16:15), and, through Jesus, it belongs to you. Hebrews 1:2 tells us that Jesus is the heir of all things. When you accepted His sacrifice, you became a child of God and a joint heir *with Him*. Romans 8:17 says, "And if children, then heirs; heirs of God, and joint-heirs with Christ...." You share His covenant with the Father! Romans 8:29 tells us, "For whom he did foreknow, he also did predestinate to be conformed to the image of his Son, that he might be the firstborn among many brethren."

When you accepted Jesus' sacrifice, you became a new creature, born again in the image of Jesus. The old covenant offered physical well-being with a promise of spiritual success, but the new covenant instantly brings about a new man who is the very righteousness of God Himself (2 Corinthians 5:17, 21)!

Your new spirit has eternal life and is *immediately* a spiritual success. Your mind and body may not realize it, but the sin nature that kept you from the presence of God is gone, once and for all.

You now have a personal invitation to come, at will, into the Father's presence—not only to come but also to receive. You have a covenant with Him! Hebrews 4:16 says, "Let us therefore come boldly unto the throne of grace, that we may obtain mercy, and find grace to help in time of need."

LEARN YOUR COVENANT

If you are in Christ, you have a covenant with Almighty God. You may not know how to take advantage of what God has agreed to do for you, but nevertheless, the new covenant provisions belong to you.

Kenneth and I have spent many years diligently studying our covenant. I am sharing with you the truths we've learned that made us free. As we learned what our covenant provides in the area of healing and began to act uncompromisingly on that provision, sickness had to bow its knee. We have opportunities to be sick, but *we pass them by!* Instead, we hold fast to our covenant rights, and as we steadfastly adhere to God's WORD, He fulfills His covenant with us.

Before we knew we had a covenant with God, we were just like everyone else. Sickness and defeat were with us continually, and we were subject to them. *Freedom belonged to us, but we didn't know our spiritual Bill of Rights—the New Testament.*

Now, we know through The WORD, Jesus purchased our complete deliverance from Satan's evil work. By diligently acting on our covenant with God, we stopped Satan's manipulation of our lives and opened wide the door of God's BLESSING.

Are you beginning to see what has held believers in bondage? They have not known their covenant. "Therefore my people are gone into captivity, because they have no knowledge" (Isaiah 5:13).

The majority of Christians know only that God has given them salvation and that heaven will be their home—the only provisions of the covenant they have enjoyed. But God has provided healing, peace that passes all understanding and prosperity—all benefits that are yours, just as surely as the new birth.

In the new covenant, God is telling you, just as He told Abraham, that He has already made provision for your success in every area of life.

The more you study and learn your covenant with God, the more you will walk worthy of Him because the wonderful things God has given you will be manifest in your life. But you will not be able to receive beyond your knowledge of the covenant because you will only be able to confidently lay hold of the provisions you know are His will. Because God's WORD is His covenant with you, you'll now have something concrete on which to base your life. This is one of the wonderful things about The WORD of God. It is a never-changing standard that always works.

Deuteronomy 32:4 says of The LORD: "He is the Rock, His work is perfect, for all His ways are law and justice. A God of faithfulness without breach or deviation, just and right is He" *(The Amplified Bible)*. Hebrews 13:8 says, "Jesus Christ [is] the same yesterday, and to day, and for ever."

The more you abide in this Rock and in His WORD, the more stable and immovable you become. To the people around you, you'll begin to look like a rock. You'll begin to be the light of Jesus in a dark world. When someone comes to you in need, you can point him to the portion of God's WORD that provides the answer to his problem. You become dependable, victorious and the one who has the answer.

I have seen the most helpless and weak people become this kind of rock in the eyes of their neighbors, family and friends. One friend was near a nervous breakdown with thoughts of committing suicide. Then, she began finding out things about God she had never known. She received the Baptism in the Holy Spirit and began to study The WORD, reading it simply as God speaking to her. She read it, not as a history book, but as the Book that contained answers for her. Her faith began to work as she learned to rely and act on God's WORD. She began to look like a rock to other people.

Eventually, a man of stature in the eyes of the world, who walks with influence among the great people of our nation, told her that he wanted what she had. She is a homemaker, but through The WORD, she had learned how to be strong in The LORD. She shared with him what had made the change in her life, and now, *he* is a new man with a hunger for God's WORD. As he learns his covenant, he too, will begin to look like a rock to those in need!

Psalm 112 is the picture of the person you can become. Take God's WORD for it. Note the condition spoken of in verse 1 that brings about these great results. This man fears (reveres or regards with deep and affectionate respect) The LORD, and He delights in His covenant (or WORD)! He never worries or becomes desperate. He trusts in The LORD and is steadfast and sure. He is the man everyone would like to be.

> Praise ye The LORD. BLESSED is the man that feareth The LORD, that delighteth greatly in his command-ments. His seed shall be mighty upon earth: the genera-tion of the upright shall be blessed. Wealth and riches shall be in his house: and his righteousness endureth for ever. Unto the upright there ariseth light in the darkness: he is gracious, and full of compassion, and righteous. A good man showeth favour, and lendeth: he will guide his affairs with discretion. Surely he shall not be moved for

ever: the righteous shall be in everlasting remembrance.
He shall not be afraid of evil tidings: his heart is fixed,
trusting in The LORD. His heart is established, he shall
not be afraid, until he see his desire upon his enemies.
He hath dispersed, he hath given to the poor; his righteousness endureth for ever; his horn shall be exalted
with honour. The wicked shall see it, and be grieved; he
shall gnash with his teeth, and melt away: the desire of
the wicked shall perish.

This should energize and create a desire in you to find out what your
covenant with God says.

FAITH COMES BY THE WORD

"Hebrews 11:6 says, "But without faith it is impossible to please him:
for he that cometh to God must believe that he is, and that he is a rewarder
of them that diligently seek him." Since it is impossible to please God
without faith, there is no doubt that God's will is not only for you to have it
but also for you to live by it. Hebrews 10:38 says, "Now the just shall live by
faith: but if any man draw back, my soul shall have no pleasure in him."

Every believer desires to please God. If it is necessary for you to have
faith to please God, you know that our just God has provided that faith
for you and will teach you how to use it.

Everyone does not have faith. Second Thessalonians 3:2 says, "And that
we may be delivered from unreasonable and wicked men: *for all men have
not faith.*" When Adam was born again from life to death, fear replaced
the faith God had originally created in Adam. Natural man became void of
faith. "I was afraid" are the first words Adam spoke to God after he sinned.

Who, then, has faith? In writing to the church at Rome, Paul said
that God has dealt to every man the measure of faith (Romans 12:3).
Every born-again person has faith.

When you became a new creature in Christ, all spiritual things were made new (2 Corinthians 5:17). Your new spirit was re-created in the image of God. Ephesians 4:24 says, "And that ye put on the new man, which after God is created in righteousness and true holiness." Eternal life replaced spiritual death. The righteousness of God replaced sin, the God-kind of love replaced your selfishness and God's faith replaced your fear.

Ephesians 2:8 says you are saved through faith; and that it is the gift of God! You have faith—that is how you got saved. God gave you *His* faith, and He has not taken it back. It is not human faith but God's faith—it is the gift of God.

You have the same faith God used when His words created this world (Hebrews 11:3). Jesus said if you have faith, you can remove a mountain with your words and nothing is impossible to you (Matthew 17:20). In you dwells the God-kind of faith.

What brought this faith into your life?

Romans 10:14, 17 says, "How then shall they call on him in whom they have not believed? and how shall they believe in him of whom they have not heard? and how shall they hear without a preacher?... So then faith cometh by hearing, and hearing by The WORD of God."

Faith came by hearing what Jesus did for you when He suffered sin's penalty in your place and arose from the dead, victorious. When you heard this good news, faith came to you to receive Him as Savior and LORD. When you acted on that WORD and confessed Him as LORD, you were re-created. God's powerful faith came into your heart to remain forever.

The WORD—His covenant—is the source of faith. Faith cometh by hearing The WORD. Faith receives by acting on The WORD.

The faith that abides in the new creature is exercised through obedience to the conditions of the covenant. Salvation, then, is received by obeying the conditions of the covenant (The WORD) in the area of salvation. Healing is received by obeying the conditions of the covenant (The WORD) in the area of healing.

"Now faith is the substance of things hoped for, the evidence of things not seen" (Hebrews 11:1). Faith acts on The WORD, *now*. It is never in the future. If it is not now, it is not faith. Faith gives substance. It brings the things we hope for into a now reality. Faith is evidence of things not seen.

God's WORD is faith's evidence. All faith needs to know is that God has spoken. It asks for no evidence other than the written WORD of God.

As you grow in the spirit, every step you take comes as you hear God's WORD with your spiritual ears and act on it. All spiritual growth comes by revelation of The WORD.

Many Christians become indignant when you tell them they are wasting time praying for faith. Nevertheless, God says faith comes—*will* come—by hearing The WORD, not by prayer. Prayer does not cause faith to work, faith causes prayer to work.

One day, I found in the Bible, that God cared for me. I believed that WORD and acted on it by asking Him to take my life and do something with it. Later, I heard He sent the Holy Spirit to me. I acted on what I heard and received Him to dwell in me.

I also heard that Jesus not only took my sin on Himself, but on the same day, He bore my diseases. The Bible says I have been redeemed from sickness. Then, why should I be sick? No sickness has been able to stay in my body since I learned that The WORD provided healing for me. *What God says in His WORD causes faith to come into your heart.*

Faith is in you. Now, it must be developed in specific areas by The WORD. Faith comes from The WORD—The WORD brings it forth. As you hear God's WORD on healing, faith rises to receive it.

Determine to learn the conditions and the provisions of the covenant you have with Almighty God!

THE FORCES OF FAITH

Faith is a spiritual force. It makes a demand on the power of God and receives the desired result. When two blind men came to the Master, Jesus said to them, "Believe ye that I am able to do this? They said unto him, Yea, LORD. Then touched he their eyes, saying, According to your faith be it unto you. And their eyes were opened" (Matthew 9:28-30). Their faith made a demand on the power of God to open their eyes.

A woman suffered with an issue of blood for 12 years. She could find no cure. She heard of Jesus and made her way to Him, saying, "If I may touch but his clothes, I shall be whole" (Mark 5:28). Her faith was speaking. The moment she touched Jesus' garment, she was healed. The woman made a demand on the power of God. Jesus realized that power had gone out of Him and asked, "Who touched my clothes?" (verse 30). The power was already going out of Jesus to meet her need *before* He knew who touched Him.

What caused the power of God to go into her body and stop the flow of blood? Jesus said unto her, "Daughter, thy *faith* hath made thee whole" (verse 34).

Faith is the spiritual force that causes the supernatural intervention of God's power to come into a body, a life, a circumstance. Anyone exerting this force of faith could have received. It was not the woman's righteous character that caused power to flow, nor was it her ability to influence. It was the force of faith.

THE WORD IS SPIRIT FOOD

Man is a spirit, he has a soul and he lives in a body. All three must be properly nourished for them to operate successfully. The physical body feeds on physical food to gain and maintain its strength. It goes into the body and becomes part of it.

Your soul feeds on intellectual food which produces willpower. Feeding your soul on nothing but television and other mental candy will manifest little willpower. Your mind must be trained and developed to produce intellectual strength.

Your spirit feeds and gains its power from spirit food. Jesus said, "The WORDS that I speak unto you, they are spirit, and they are life" (John 6:63). God's WORDS are spirit. If you do not feed the man on the inside with spiritual food, he will become weaker and weaker.

To exert spiritual power, you must feed your spirit on The WORD of God with the same faithfulness as you feed your body. God told Joshua to meditate in His WORD day and night. Great spiritual power was the result.

When you put God's WORD into your spirit—or heart—it is consumed by your spirit, becoming part of it and producing the spiritual force called *faith*.

This force of faith is so powerful that Jesus said a little measure the size of a mustard seed is enough to blast a mountain into the sea. Even with this small amount of faith, He said nothing would be impossible to you (Matthew 17:20).

God said in Isaiah 55:11, "So shall My WORD be that goes forth out of My mouth: it shall not return to Me void [without producing any effect, useless] but it shall accomplish that which I please and purpose, and it shall prosper in the thing for which I sent it" *(The Amplified Bible)*.

God's WORDS are powerful faith words. They go into your heart to bring forth after their own kind and produce faith words in your mouth. Faith is released by words. God's WORD in your mouth will bring to pass His will in your life. His WORD, spoken through the lips of a believer, with the force of faith behind it, accomplishes whatever that WORD proclaims. Jesus said, "For verily I say unto you, That whosoever shall say unto this mountain, Be thou removed, and be thou cast into the sea; and shall not doubt in his heart, but shall believe that those things which he saith shall come to pass; *he shall have whatsoever he saith*" (Mark 11:23).

You cannot believe one thing, say another and then expect to receive what you *think* you believe. What you say with your mouth is what you believe in your heart. Your mouth matches your faith.

GOD'S WORD IN YOUR MOUTH WILL BRING TO PASS HIS WILL IN YOUR LIFE.

If you have a weak, negative confession, your spirit is suffering from a severe case of malnutrition. There is no cure for that except feeding on spirit food—The WORD of God, until you become like the man in Psalm 1:2-3: "His delight is in the law of The LORD; and in his law doth he meditate day and night. And he shall be like a tree planted by the rivers of water, that bringeth forth his fruit in his season; his leaf also shall not wither; and whatsoever he doeth shall prosper."

SCRIPTURE:

"...that ye might be filled with the knowledge of his will in all wisdom and spiritual understanding" (Colossians 1:9).

POINTS TO REMEMBER:

1. The WORD is God speaking to you, teaching you how to live an abundant and successful life.

2. Give The WORD first place in your schedule, and everything else will come into agreement with God's will for your life.

3. His WORD is forever settled in heaven. When we speak of God's WORD, we are not speaking of a book. This Book is The WORD of God written down. It is His bond—His integrity.

4. All these provisions God offered Israel—wealth, protection, health and success—are *yours through Jesus.* "And if ye be Christ's, then are ye Abraham's seed, and heirs according to the promise" (Galatians 3:29). It is an everlasting agreement.

5. When you put God's WORD into your spirit, it produces the spiritual force called faith.

CONFESSION:

God's WORD is His will. It is supernatural and alive. It is God speaking to me. I highly value God's WORD and put it first place in my life. It makes me victorious in all I do. It is my reference Book for living. According to Joshua 1:8, I meditate on God's WORD day and night, and I fearlessly act on what it says, knowing that no word from God is without power. Therefore, I deal wisely and have good success in all I do. God's WORD is my supreme authority and its wisdom opens the door for God's higher way of life for me. I am a covenant believer, and I walk in THE BLESSING of Abraham. God meets my every need. I never worry or become desperate because I trust in the truth of His WORD.

CHAPTER FOUR

God's Will Is Healing

You must *know* it is God's will to heal you. Until this fact is settled in your mind and spirit, you cannot approach healing without being double-minded and wavering. The Scripture states the double-minded man will receive nothing from The LORD (James 1:6-8).

The WORD of God must abide in you concerning your healing. You have a covenant with God that includes divine health—every Christian does. The problem has been that most Christians don't know healing belongs to them. The Holy Spirit, by the prophet Hosea says, "My people are destroyed for lack of knowledge" (Hosea 4:6). In the realm of healing, this scripture is continually being fulfilled.

Christians have allowed disease and sickness to destroy their bodies, when all the while God's WORD says that by His stripes you were healed (1 Peter 2:24). They are being physically destroyed because of ignorance of The WORD concerning their healing.

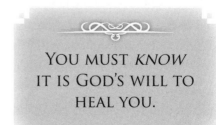

YOU MUST *KNOW* IT IS GOD'S WILL TO HEAL YOU.

THE WORD IS THE SEED

Jesus teaches in the parable of the sower that *The WORD of God is the seed,* and the hearts of men are the ground (Mark 4:14-20). The faith seed of The WORD concerning your healing must be planted in you before you can successfully reap the healing harvest.

"Being born again, not of corruptible seed, but of incorruptible, by The WORD of God, which liveth and abideth for ever" (1 Peter 1:23). The WORD of God is the *incorruptible* seed. It cannot be spoiled by disease or any other force Satan has to offer. The WORD cannot even be weakened. Forever, God's WORD will have life and power.

This incorruptible seed worked when you were born again. The WORD concerning salvation went into your heart and produced the faith to be saved.

Faith comes for healing in the same way—by hearing The WORD concerning healing. "So then faith cometh by hearing, and hearing by The WORD of God" (Romans 10:17).

There is no substitute for the seed—not even prayer. Faith comes by hearing The WORD, and no other way. Praying for faith misses the mark because God has already dealt to every born-again man the measure of faith (Romans 12:3). You received the faith of God when you were born again.

By hearing The WORD, you continue to develop your faith in specific areas. As you study The WORD concerning healing, the force of faith rises up in you to receive God's healing power in your body.

All Christians have had the seed of salvation sown in their hearts. They have no trouble believing they are saved and will go to heaven because most of the sermons preached are about salvation. That seed has been well-planted, cultivated and watered. When asked, "Is your name written in the Lamb's Book of Life?" without hesitation or doubt, most will say, "Yes, it is!" Have they ever seen the book? No, but they have confidence in this area because they have been taught that their name is written there. Though they have not seen the book, they believe. That is faith in operation.

Faith should be as highly developed in the Church concerning healing as it is for salvation.

If the Church had been told what The WORD says about healing, Christians would be equally as quick to believe they are healed. However, instead of teaching and preaching that healing belongs to Christians, many have been taught against it.

It is easy to understand then, why the Church of Jesus Christ as a whole has not walked in divine health, even though for all these years it has belonged to us.

The seeds of doubt and unbelief have been sown by traditions that came as a result of men trying to teach God's WORD through head knowledge rather than by His Spirit. Jesus said that men make the commandment of God of no effect by their tradition (Matthew 15:6).

One tradition, for example, tells us that healing has passed away—that it was just for the early Church in order to get them started. Another tradition says that God heals some people but you never know if He will heal you.

THE THORN IN THE FLESH

Tradition also teaches that Paul's "thorn in the flesh " (2 Corinthians 12:7) was sickness or disease, though The WORD plainly tells us this thorn was a messenger *from Satan*—a personality. (God does not use Satan's messengers. He has His own messenger service!) The word for *messenger* is also translated in other verses of the New Testament as *angel*.

Watch this messenger of Satan deal Paul blow after blow in the following scriptures: "But when the Jews saw the multitudes, they were filled with envy, and spake against those things which were spoken by Paul, contradicting and blaspheming.... But the Jews stirred up the devout and honourable women, and the chief men of the city, and raised persecution against Paul and Barnabas, and expelled them out of their coasts" (Acts 13:45, 50).

After this incident at Antioch, the apostles shook the dust from their feet and went into Iconium. They spoke boldly in The LORD, and He gave testimony to The WORD by granting signs and wonders to be done by their hands.

> And when there was an assault made both of the Gentiles, and also of the Jews with their rulers, to use them despitefully, and to stone them, they were ware of it, and fled unto Lystra.... And there came thither certain Jews from Antioch and Iconium, who persuaded the people, and, having stoned Paul, drew him out of the city, supposing he had been dead. Howbeit, as the disciples stood round about him, he rose up, and came into the city: and the next day he departed with Barnabas to Derbe (Acts 14:5-6, 19-20).

The envious men from Antioch and Iconium brought the persecution against Paul to Lystra, but they were only instruments used by the source of persecution—the messenger of Satan. Wherever Paul went, the evil spirit worked to incite the people against him. *This evil messenger was a thorn in Paul's side!*

The LORD told Moses that if the Israelites did not drive out the inhabitants of the land of Canaan, those inhabitants would vex them and be "pricks in their eyes and thorns in their sides" (Numbers 33:55). In the same way, Paul himself describes this evil angel as a thorn in his side: "There was given me a thorn in the flesh, Satan's angel to torture me" (2 Corinthians 12:7, *Weymouth*).

An evil spirit was assigned to Paul to stop The WORD from being preached. Paul had received an abundance of revelation, and Satan came to snatch that WORD away (Mark 4:15). Satan will see to it that no believer is exalted above the measure of The WORD that actually lives in him. The WORD that is alive in you is The WORD that you steadfastly act on. You will have to stand in faith for every word of revelation knowledge you receive. God had given Paul the revelation of the authority of the believer. He had authority over Satan, in the Name of Jesus, just as you do. To get results, *Paul had to enforce this authority* by directly commanding the evil spirit to desist in his maneuvers against him.

"For this thing I besought The LORD thrice, that it might depart from me" (2 Corinthians 12:8). If you want results, don't ask God to deal with the devil for you. Just as God told Moses to drive out the inhabitants of the land, He instructs *you* to drive out the demons or evil spirits (Mark 16:17). "Submit yourselves therefore to God. Resist the devil, and he will flee from you" (James 4:7).

God has given you the Name of Jesus and the authority to use that Name in binding Satan and his forces. God will not deal with Satan for you, but when you take the Name of Jesus and The WORD of God and command him to stop his attack against you, all of heaven *guarantees* results. Paul himself writes by the Spirit in Ephesians 6:12, "For we wrestle not against flesh and blood, but against principalities, against powers, against the rulers of the darkness of this world, against spiritual wickedness in high places." We wrestle against these evil spirits. Speak directly to Satan and his evil spirits in the Name of Jesus, and cast them out!

When Paul asked The LORD that this messenger of Satan depart from him, The LORD said, "My grace is sufficient for thee: for my strength is made perfect in weakness" (2 Corinthians 12:9). *He did not say that the messenger would not depart.* He was saying to Paul, "My favor is enough. For when you do not have the ability to humanly overcome, you use *My* Name to stop Satan's attack, and My power will excel in your behalf. My favor is enough. *You* cast out the devil." The Greek word *dunamis* translated *strength* in 2 Corinthians 12:9 is the same word translated *power* when Jesus said, "Ye shall receive power, after that the

Holy Ghost is come upon you" (Acts 1:8). The more literal translation
is *power.* The *Weymouth* translation reads, "My grace suffices for you,
for power is perfected in weakness."[3] (This is the opposite of traditional
teaching that Paul had no victory over the thorn in the flesh.)

Then Paul said, "Most gladly therefore will I rather glory in my infirmities, that the power of Christ may rest upon me. Therefore I take pleasure
in infirmities, in reproaches, in necessities, in persecutions, in distresses
for Christ's sake: for when I am weak, then am I strong" (2 Corinthians
12:9-10). The Greek word translated *infirmities* means "want of strength,
weakness, indicating inability to produce results."[4] Paul lists these buffet-
ings—imprisonments, stoning, beatings, shipwrecks and angry mobs—in
detail in 2 Corinthians 11:23-28. *Sickness is not mentioned.*

When the mob came after Paul to stone him, he had no strength in
himself nor power to overcome the situation. Twice The LORD's grace
proved sufficient, and he escaped out of their hands.

In Lystra, they actually stoned Paul. Thinking he was dead, they took
him out of the city. But God had said, *My grace is sufficient for thee,* and as
the disciples stood around him, he rose up and went on his way. Paul had
no strength to stop that angry mob, but when he was humanly helpless,
God's power was displayed mightily and wrought a great deliverance for
him. Though Paul was not strong in himself, he was strong in The LORD
and in the power of His might.

Satan's angel, the thorn in the flesh, could gain no victory over Paul
through adverse circumstances because the power of Christ rested upon
him. He said, "I have learned in any and all circumstances, the secret of
facing every situation" (Philippians 4:12, *The Amplified Bible).* In the
next verse, Paul shares this secret: "I have strength for all things in Christ

---

3   Richard Francis Weymouth, *The New Testament in Modern Speech* (Fort Worth:
     Kenneth Copeland Publications, 1996).

4   Vine, W.E., *An Expository Dictionary of Biblical Words,* (Old Tappan, N.J.:
     Fleming H. Revell Company, 1966) Vol. II, p. 257.

Who empowers me [I am ready for anything and equal to anything through Him Who infuses inner strength into me...]."

When Paul in himself was weak, Paul in Christ was strong. Of these afflictions and persecutions Paul wrote to Timothy: "Persecutions, sufferings—such as occurred to me at Antioch, at Iconium, and at Lystra, persecutions I endured, but out of them all The LORD delivered me" (2 Timothy 3:11, *The Amplified Bible*).

The LORD delivered the Apostle Paul out of them *all!* He lived to be an old man and then said in Philippians 1:23 that he could not decide whether to stay here or to go be with The LORD. He decided he needed to stay for the Church's sake but yearned to go be with Jesus. Paul did not leave this world until he and The LORD were ready. Satan's angel, the thorn in the flesh that we have heard so much about, never did overcome Paul and the power of God. Satan could do no more than vex him and be a thorn in his flesh. But Paul was a covenant man. He ran the race and won. He preached The WORD around the known world, wrote most of the New Testament, and caused revival wherever he went. When human strength ends, the power of God excels.

Paul's thorn in the flesh is just another tradition that Satan has used to deceive and rob the Church.

Another tradition says that God gets glory from sickness because the world sees how marvelously the Christian bears the pain and agony. (Tradition never adds up to the right answer.) Anyone knows that the world has all the pain and agony it can stand. What the world wants is a way *out* of sickness—not a way into it. Suffering has no appeal to the world, but through tradition, Satan has sold it to the Church as being the will of God.

How helpless you are in the face of Satan and disease without The WORD of God living in you concerning your healing!

If you allow the traditions of men to usurp authority over God's WORD, you will continue to be helpless in the face of sickness. God will not be able to do anything for you—*you* have made The WORD "of none effect" in your life.

The WORD of God is the incorruptible seed. Satan does not have the power to stop it. Disease does not have the power to overcome it. Only you have the power to stop The WORD from working in your life.

Lay aside what tradition has taught you. Your heart has never agreed with it, anyway! Realize that only Satan could be the source of such powerless, defeated beliefs sold to the family of Almighty God.

As you study The WORD of God concerning healing, this incorruptible seed of The WORD will drive out the doubt and tradition you have been taught.

FIRST PLANT THE SEED

Many try to reap the healing harvest without first planting the seed. "Until the person seeking healing is sure from God's WORD that it is God's will to heal him, he is trying to reap a harvest where there is no seed planted."[5]

Can you imagine a farmer at planting time sitting down on his front porch and saying, "I'm going to believe for a crop this year. I believe in crops and know that they are real. So I will not plant the seed. I'll just believe"?

Unless the farmer plants the seed, he has *no basis for faith.* No matter how hard he tries to believe, there is nothing in the ground to produce the harvest.

Even if you believe in healing, without the healing seed of God's WORD planted in you, there is nothing in the ground to produce the harvest. You have no real basis for faith. Neither you nor the farmer will reap the harvest unless you first plant the seed.

Believing in healing is not enough. You must *know* that it is God's will for *you* to be healed.

Allow the faith seed of The WORD of God concerning your healing

---

5   Bosworth, F.F., *Christ the Healer* (Grand Rapids: Fleming H. Revell, 1973) p. 6.

to be planted in you, and you'll successfully reap the healing harvest.

Through The WORD, you can know without a doubt that it is God's unchanging will for you to be healed.

A STUDY OF THE HEART

"And the very God of peace sanctify you wholly; and I pray God your whole spirit and soul and body be preserved blameless unto the coming of our LORD Jesus Christ" (1 Thessalonians 5:23).

Man is a spirit. He has a soul, made up of his reasoning faculties, will and emotions; and he lives in a physical body.

The heart of man is the spirit of man. Your spirit is the real you. (Do you have a human? No, you *are* a human. You do not have a spirit. You *are* a spirit.)

Man thinks of himself as being only a body because he cannot see his spirit with the natural eye. But to understand spiritual things, it is important you realize *you are a spirit.*

This "new creature" or the "hidden man of the heart," as the Scripture calls him, is the spirit—the real man. This is the part of you that is re-created in the righteousness of God when you are born again. Your mind and body are not made new, but *you* (the hidden man) are re-created. Second Corinthians 5:17 says, "Therefore if any man be in Christ, he is a new creature: old things are passed away; behold, all things are become new."

"But let it be the hidden man of the heart, in that which is not corruptible, even the ornament of a meek and quiet spirit, which is in the sight of God of great price" (1 Peter 3:4).

Paul speaks of the body as "the clothing of the spirit" and "the tent which is our earthly home" (2 Corinthians 5:1-8, *The Amplified Bible).* Your body is a covering for your spirit.

In the same text, Paul speaks of being absent from the body and being present with The LORD. When the man (the spirit) leaves the body, the body dies. The spirit is the life of the body. The spirit can live without the body, but the body cannot live without the spirit.

The spirit does not die. The spirit of man will live forever—either with his god Satan or with The LORD Jesus Christ. When a man dies, he does not cease to exist. He only ceases to live in the physical body.

The spirit is called "the heart" of a man because it is the core or center of his being. The heart of a tree is the core of that tree. The heart of a watermelon is the center of the melon, not an organ that pumps watermelon juice! Whenever the Scripture speaks of the heart, it is not speaking of the physical blood pump but the real man—or the spirit.

THE HEART OF MAN IS THE GROUND

The Scripture tells us that God provides seed for the sower (2 Corinthians 9:10). He has already given you the incorruptible seed—The WORD of God.

Not only has He provided you with the seed, but He has also prepared the ground. The heart of man is the ground where the seed of The WORD is planted. When you were born again by His Holy Spirit, your heart was created in His image, "And that ye put on the new man, which after God is created in righteousness and true holiness" (Ephesians 4:24).

At one time, your heart was corrupt. You had the nature of spiritual death and could only produce sin. Now you are a new man, created in God's image.

"For he hath made him to be sin for us, who knew no sin; that we might be made the righteousness of God in him" (2 Corinthians 5:21). God paid a great price to make you good ground for His WORD. Through the sacrifice of His Son, Jesus, He has made you the righteousness of God.

The good ground of your heart was created by His power to be the dwelling place for His Spirit and His WORD. Not only that, but the force of faith was born into this new creature.

If you have been born again, you have faith. You may not have known how to use it, but faith has been born into you. It is the same faith God used to create the world. The WORD—the seed—brings forth fruit by this same force issuing from the heart.

Jesus teaches us some very important things concerning the good ground of the heart and the seed of The WORD.

SATAN STEALS THE WORD

"The sower soweth The WORD. And these are they by the way side, where The WORD is sown; but when they have heard, Satan cometh immediately, and taketh away The WORD that was sown in their hearts" (Mark 4:14-15).

In this parable, notice that The WORD was sown, and it worked. It went into the heart. It is the incorruptible seed and would have produced after its kind, but the hearers allowed Satan to take it out of their hearts.

Satan snatches The WORD away through persecution, doubt, unbelief and tradition. He does everything in his power to keep The WORD from abiding in your heart in order to keep you nonproductive. In the parable, the seed was taken out of the ground. It could, therefore, produce no harvest and Satan's work continued, unhindered.

STONY GROUND

"And these are they likewise which are sown on stony ground; who, when they have heard The WORD, immediately receive it with gladness; and have no root in themselves, and so endure but for a time: afterward, when affliction or persecution ariseth for The WORD's sake, immediately they are offended" (verses 16-17).

The stony ground did not allow the seed to take root. These people believed The WORD until trouble came. Then they had no confidence to act on The WORD—it had no root. When feelings or circumstances looked contrary to The WORD that was sown, these people let The WORD go and believed what they could see.

When you receive revelation knowledge from The WORD, Satan

will test and try you in order to get The WORD out of your heart. There is no way the seed can produce fruit unless it is in the ground. The WORD is no threat to Satan until it is put into the heart of man.

Notice, this verse said affliction came because of The WORD. When you receive The WORD on healing, Satan will attempt to make you sick so you will be offended and let go of The WORD that was put in your heart.

He will try to make you sick, but he can't if you will resist him. However, *if you allow yourself* to be stony ground, when trouble comes, you will be offended and fall away from The WORD. You will let The WORD wither away in your heart before it can take root.

THORNS IN THE HEART

"And these are they which are sown among thorns; such as hear The WORD, and the cares of this world, and the deceitfulness of riches, and the lusts of other things entering in, choke The WORD, and it becometh unfruitful" (verses 18-19).

Beware of the thorns of life. The cares of this world, deceitfulness of riches and the lusts of other things are dangerous strategies of the enemy. They enter into the heart and choke The WORD until it cannot produce.

People in this category have given their thoughts, life and energy to the cares of this world, running after riches and the lusts of their flesh. They have set their minds on and pursue things that gratify the flesh. The Scripture teaches that the mind of the flesh is death (Romans 8:5-6). Theirs is an overcrowded heart. Yes, The WORD is in there. They are "WORD" people but there are so many other things in their hearts that The WORD is unfruitful. It cannot accomplish what it was sent from heaven to do. Isaiah 55:11 says, "So shall my WORD be that goeth forth out of my mouth: it shall not return unto me void, but it shall accomplish that which I please, and it shall prosper in the thing whereto I sent it."

Thorns in the heart are deadly.

This is the direct opposite from what God told Joshua to do in order to make his way prosperous and have good success. He told Joshua to meditate in His WORD day and night—to set his mind on The WORD.

You, like Joshua, are admonished to set your affections on things that are above and not on things that are on the earth (Colossians 3:2). Oh, yes! This is to your great advantage because to be spiritually minded is life and peace (Romans 8:6). You have God's WORD that when you seek first His kingdom, all these other things will be added to you (Matthew 6:33).

The same formula God gave to Joshua still works today (Joshua 1:8). God has given the formula for success. He has given the seed and prepared the ground of your heart to receive the seed. But you must use the formula.

You set your affections. This is a matter of your will. *You* set your mind on those things which gratify your flesh (five senses), or you set your mind on those things which gratify the spirit. God *cannot* do that part for you.

Notice, it was not the ground that prevented The WORD from bearing fruit in any of these illustrations, but the things that were allowed *in* the ground—Satan, the stones and the thorns.

Give The WORD first place in your life to be good ground!

GOOD GROUND

"And these are they which are sown on good ground; such as hear The WORD, and receive it, and bring forth fruit, some thirtyfold, some sixty, and some an hundred" (Mark 4:20).

You have learned from the previous scriptures what will keep your heart from being good ground. Now, Jesus teaches how to be good ground for The WORD, thereby producing the harvest of results.

The WORD of God is the will of God. When The WORD is planted in good ground—free from hindrances—the crop that is produced will be God's will for your life.

The law of Genesis is that everything brings forth after its own kind. Plant The WORD of God in your heart, water and cultivate it, and it will bring forth the fulfillment of that WORD in your life.

Look at the hearts that were called stony ground. They heard The WORD and received it with joy. *But that was not enough!* When trouble came, they had no confidence in what they had heard. They

FAITH IS ACTING ON GOD'S WORD, REGARDLESS OF WHAT YOU SEE.

were moved by what they saw rather than by The WORD of God. Circumstances scorched the seed, and it withered away before it could take root. Good ground hears The WORD, understands it and then acts on it.

Bringing forth fruit is acting on The WORD. Acting on The WORD germinates the seed, which causes it to sprout and take root.

Faith is acting on God's WORD, regardless of what you see—it brings forth the crop.

When trouble comes, you must hold fast to God's WORD. It is the man who will hold fast to his confession of The WORD in the hard places—in the crisis—who will obtain faith's results.

Acting on The WORD makes the difference between stony ground and good ground.

The soil brings forth *before* the crop is harvested. You are the good ground. You must act on The WORD before you see the results. "For we walk by faith, not by sight" (2 Corinthians 5:7).

Jesus said, "Therefore I say unto you, What things soever ye desire, when ye pray, believe that ye receive them, and ye shall have them" (Mark 11:24).

Believe you receive *when you pray* and *before you see* because God's WORD says the answer belongs to you. And according to Jesus, you shall have what you desire from the Father.

The heart that is good ground *hears* The WORD, *receives* The WORD and *does* The WORD.

Jesus tells us the thrilling result of the seed of The WORD planted in good ground: "If ye abide in me, and my words abide in you, ye shall ask what ye will, and it shall be done unto you" (John 15:7).

I Am The LORD That Healeth Thee

Healing was not introduced during the ministry of Jesus, nor is it only part of the New Covenant BLESSING. This may come as a surprise to many who are trying to believe that God wants to heal them, but God has always provided healing for His people through His covenants.

In the Old Covenant, He revealed Himself as the Great Physician when He told Israel that if they would obey His WORD, none of the diseases of Egypt would come upon them. He said, "For I am The LORD that healeth thee" (Exodus 15:26).

When God gave Israel THE BLESSING of the Law, He said if they would hearken diligently to the voice of The LORD and be careful to do His commandments that THE BLESSING would come upon them and overtake them.

He placed Himself as Israel's Healer—Jehovah-Rapha.

Healing was not an automatic blessing but conditional to diligently obeying His WORD.

"Fools because of their transgression, and because of their iniquities, are afflicted.... They cry unto The LORD in their trouble, and he saveth them out of their distresses. He sent His WORD, and healed them, and delivered them from their destructions" (Psalm 107:17, 19-20).

Disease came through disobedience to the Law. Forgiveness for that disobedience brought healing for their bodies. God had provided an umbrella of protection and BLESSING for His people through His WORD. When Israel sinned, they broke the covenant and took themselves out from under its protection.

As long as Israel kept the covenant with God, there was no disease powerful enough to come upon them. When they turned away from

God's WORD, disease filled their bodies.

When Israel, through disobedience, got out from under God's protection, the curse that was *already* on the earth overtook them. The whole world was under the curse that came when Adam changed gods, and Satan became his ruler.

All Israel had to do was to be like the other nations and the curse would come upon them. Without acting on God's WORD, Israel became helpless in the face of poverty, sickness, fear and her enemies.

THE ORIGIN OF SICKNESS

Our Father is the God of love and, from the beginning, has desired freedom for His people from the curse that came on the earth when Adam committed high treason.

Adam had been a free man and ruler of the earth. God had given him this domain and Adam, by an act of his own will, made Satan lord and father over him.

The nature of spiritual death replaced God's life in Adam's spirit. Sickness came into this world order on the wings of spiritual death. Man was not sick before he died spiritually.

Adam's sin was not God's will—neither are the results of that sin God's will. Satan, through the Fall of Man, is the originator of the curse and all its provisions.

Sin is manifest in the spirit. Sickness is manifest in the body. Both are the result of Satan and the rulership that man committed to him in the Fall. Both are works of evil. Neither are from the hand of God.

If God's will had been sickness and death, He would have placed them in the Garden Himself. He would not have brought sickness or sin by the hand of His enemy.

For the first time, many can see why it was necessary for Israel to diligently hearken to God's WORD. The curse was a powerful force. It had overtaken the whole world. God was not being hard or demanding or putting a burden on His people through His statutes and ordinances. But, only a power greater than the evil could stop the effect of the curse. That power is The WORD of God.

The keeping of God's covenant was Israel's *only* deliverance.

GOD IS NOT THE THIEF

It is hard for us to understand that the natural laws governing the earth largely came into being with the Fall of Man and the curse that came on the earth.

Because of this misunderstanding, many accuse God of causing the accidents, sickness, death of loved ones, storms, catastrophes, earthquakes and floods that continually occur. But, Jesus set aside all these natural laws, as we understand them, whenever it was necessary, in order to bless humanity.

Natural laws came with the Fall, their author is Satan, and when he is finally eliminated from human contact—or rather, from the earth— these laws will stop functioning.[6]

After Satan is cast into the lake of fire, there will be no tears, death, sorrow nor pain on the earth. The source of these evil works will be bound and tormented day and night forever and ever (Revelation 20:10).

"And God shall wipe away all tears from their eyes; and there shall be no more death, neither sorrow, nor crying, neither shall there be any more pain: for the former things are passed away" (Revelation 21:4).

The origin of sickness and disease is as obvious as the origin of sin. Jesus said, "The thief cometh not, but for to steal, and to kill, and to destroy: I am come that they might have life, and that they might have it more abundantly" (John 10:10).

God is not the thief! Satan has come to steal from you, kill and destroy you in any way he can. Until you find out from The WORD what belongs to you, he will continue to distress and manipulate your life.

---

6   Kenyon, E.W., *Jesus the Healer,* (Lynnwood, Wash.: Kenyon's Gospel Publishing Society, 2000) p. 51.

Most people, even Christians, blame God for Satan's work because they don't realize that it is only through the intervention of the Body of Christ in the affairs of earth that God is able to bless humanity today. First John 5:19 says, "We know [positively] that we are of God, and the whole world [around us] is under the power of the evil one" *(The Amplified Bible).*

All the authority and dominion that the Church does not actively enforce is under the sway and power of Satan—not because it is God's will, but because man originally gave Satan dominion over him. Even though Jesus has taken that dominion away from Satan, man is still in authority in the earth.

Because of our enemy, this authority does not operate passively nor automatically, but *must be enforced.* In ignorance of God's WORD, the Church has allowed Satan to steal her authority and, for the most part, to control the earth.

Jesus conquered Satan in his own domain. "And having spoiled principalities and powers, he made a show of them openly, triumphing over them in it" (Colossians 2:15).

The Amplified Bible says, "[God] disarmed the principalities and powers that were ranged against us and made a bold display and public example of them."

Weymouth says, "And the hostile princes and rulers He stripped off from Himself, and boldly displayed them as His conquests." *Weymouth* says in a footnote that *princes and rulers* are literally translated *authorities and powers.*

Jesus took by conquest all the authority that Adam had given Satan in the Fall. Jesus, the Son of God, stripped Himself and became like man and was born a human being so that, as a man, He could conquer Satan and take back from him all the authority that belonged to Adam.

Jesus incapacitated and paralyzed Satan. He has been disarmed—no weapons—where the Church is concerned. All the power and authority Satan uses in the earth now belongs to the Church of Jesus Christ.

Jesus gave the power of attorney to the Church before He ascended and sat down at the right hand of the Father. He said, "All power is given unto me in heaven and in earth. Go ye therefore..." (Matthew 28:18-19). "And these signs shall follow them that believe; In my name shall they cast out devils; they shall speak with new tongues; they shall take up serpents; and if they drink any deadly thing, it shall not hurt them; they shall lay hands on the sick, and they shall recover" (Mark 16:17-18).

Jesus said, "All power—ability to do or act—has been given to Me. Therefore, you go in My Name, and these signs shall follow you." He authorized the Church to use His Name with all its vast authority. The WORD *authorize* means "to give official approval or legal power to, or to give the right to act or to empower."

In the Great Commission, Jesus proved that in His Name believers were not limited by the natural laws that have governed the earth since Satan began to rule.

"In my name shall they cast out devils." Because the Name of Jesus has invested in it all authority in heaven and earth, the believer has the power to cast out devils. (Under the old covenant man did not have authority over Satan. Only under the protection of the Law of Moses could he enjoy any kind of freedom from distress. At that time, man did not deal with Satan directly.)

"They shall speak with new tongues." Because of Jesus' sacrifice and the coming of the Holy Spirit, natural limitations of speech have been removed. Now, the believer can talk in the spirit with The LORD. No longer limited by his lack of understanding, the new man in Christ, filled with His Spirit, can speak mysteries to his God (1 Corinthians 14:2).

"They shall take up serpents; and if they drink any deadly thing, it shall not hurt them." If a believer accidentally drinks poison or gets a snake bite, the Name of Jesus, spoken in faith, will stop the deadly effects, even though natural law says these are fatal. Record of this is seen in Paul's ministry when the deadly viper attached itself to his

hand and the natives of Malta waited for him to die (Acts 28:1-6). Natural law had no power over him because he was operating under the jurisdiction of the Name of Jesus. Death had no power to overcome this authority!

"They shall lay hands on the sick, and they shall recover." Not all the sick in the world shall recover, but those on whom the believer lays hands in the Name of Jesus. The law of sickness and disease that has worked practically unhindered since the Fall of Man must cease to operate at the command of a believer, in the Name of Jesus!

Just as in the days of old when the curse was a powerful force, it is still true today that only a power greater than the evil can stop the effect of that curse.

The Name of Jesus is greater than the curse. The WORD of God is greater than the curse. The Holy Spirit is greater than the curse. These three, mighty, supernatural forces make the believer greater and more powerful than the curse of sin, sickness, fear and poverty.

Jesus said, "I will not leave you comfortless and orphans." He kept His WORD. He sent the Holy Spirit to teach you the truths and laws of the world of the spirit, which are more powerful and supersede the natural laws that govern the earth. They do not nullify these laws, but just as the law of gravity can be superseded by the law of lift, God's laws of the Spirit are higher laws than the laws of the physical world.

God, by His Spirit, caused the Bible to be written down in man's language so man could see God's WORD with his eyes and thereby put it in his heart.

By knowledge of God's spiritual laws, the man in Christ can once again exercise authority in the earth. You have the authority of Jesus to stop the effect of the curse in your life. He said: "Verily I say unto you, Whatsoever ye shall bind on earth shall be bound in heaven: and whatsoever ye shall loose on earth shall be loosed in heaven. Again I say unto you, That if two of you shall agree on earth as touching any thing that they shall ask, it shall be done for them of my Father which is in heaven" (Matthew 18:18-19).

SHOW US THE FATHER

"Philip saith unto him, LORD, show us the Father, and it sufficeth us. Jesus saith unto him...he that hath seen me hath seen the Father.... Believest thou not that I am in the Father, and the Father in me? the words that I speak unto you I speak not of myself: but the Father that dwelleth in me, he doeth the works" (John 14:8-10).

If you want to see the Father, look at Jesus. During His ministry on Earth, Jesus revealed to men the express will of God in action. When you have seen Jesus, you have seen the Father.

Jesus did not even speak His own words. He spoke the Father's words. He did not take credit for the works that were done in His ministry but said that the Father in Him did the works.

Everything He said and did was a picture of the Father's will. Jesus said in John 8:28, *The Amplified Bible,* "...I do nothing of Myself (of My own accord or on My own authority), but I say [exactly] what My Father has taught Me." He was God's vehicle on the earth—God's way to man and man's way to God.

"For I came down from heaven, not to do mine own will, but the will of him that sent me" (John 6:38). "For this purpose the Son of God was manifested, that he might destroy the works of the devil" (1 John 3:8).

Jesus came to do God's will on the earth. His will was for Jesus to destroy the works of the devil. God set Jesus in direct opposition to Satan, the curse and all its evil effects.

Every move Jesus made and every word He spoke was geared to destroy the work of Satan. Every work of power and every healing was the will of God.

If you believe God's WORD, then you have to believe that Jesus' attitude toward sickness is God's attitude toward sickness.

JESUS THE HEALER

And great multitudes came unto him, having with them those that were lame, blind, dumb, maimed, and many others, and cast them down at Jesus' feet; and he healed them: insomuch that the multitude wondered, when they saw the dumb to speak, the maimed to be whole, the lame to walk, and the blind to see: and they glorified the God of Israel" (Matthew 15:30-31).

How God anointed Jesus of Nazareth with the Holy Ghost and with power: who went about doing good, and healing all that were oppressed of the devil; for God was with him (Acts 10:38).

And ought not this woman, being a daughter of Abraham, whom Satan hath bound, lo, these eighteen years, be loosed from this bond on the sabbath day? (Luke 13:16).

God's people were under the yoke of Satan. God sent Jesus to destroy Satan's work in their lives. He operated as a prophet under the Abrahamic covenant (Matthew 13:57). The people Jesus ministered to had a covenant of healing with God, but didn't walk in the light of it. As heirs of Abraham, they should have been free.

Jesus could not be against sin without being against sickness and disease. His Father's WORD opposed them. Therefore, Jesus opposed sickness and disease. Satan is the source of all three. You cannot be against one and not the other two.

Jesus preached deliverance to the people, and healed all who were oppressed by the devil. He taught them their covenant rights and freed them from evil spirits. He healed their bodies of sickness and disease and broke the yoke of Satan's oppression wherever He found it.

The woman who was bowed over and could not lift herself up came to Him for help. Jesus laid His hands on her and she was immediately made straight. His attitude was that this daughter of Abraham, *whom Satan had bound* for 18 years, should be loosed. This was His continual response to the people who came to Him for help.

Sickness and disease are works of Satan. Jesus, fulfilling the will of God, stopped the effect of sickness and disease at every turn. Luke 6:17-19 says, "A great multitude of people...came to hear him, and to be healed of their diseases; and they that were vexed with unclean spirits: and they were healed. And the whole multitude sought to touch him: for there went virtue out of him, and healed them all."

Jesus—the expression of God's will—*never* refused to heal anyone. Power (or virtue) was continually going forth from Him to heal all. Healing power was available to anyone who would receive it.

Jesus never asked God if it were His will to heal an individual. He knew God's attitude toward sickness. He harbored no doubt about the Father's will in healing the multitudes. The only record of anything hindering Jesus from accomplishing the will of God in the lives of His people occurred in Nazareth. Because it was His hometown, the people gave no honor to Jesus' ministry. The Bible says, "And he did not many mighty works there because of their unbelief" (Matthew 13:58).

It was not *God's* will that stopped the work but *their* wills—*their unbelief.* They were not willing to receive from the man they considered to be just the carpenter's son.

When Jesus sent His disciples out, He instructed them to "...preach the kingdom of God, and to heal the sick" (Luke 9:2). He placed no limitation on the sick—any sick were to be healed if they would receive it. He told them to freely give what they had received.

The Scriptures have shown us beyond doubt that Jesus, fulfilling the

will of God, offered healing *unconditionally* during His ministry on
the earth.

> GOD IS GOOD. HE
> COULD NOT BE THE
> SOURCE OF ANY
> SICKNESS.

Let's take one example from
Acts to demonstrate the attitude of
the early Church toward sickness.
(Note: The early Church and the
Body of Christ today, made up of
all born-again believers, is still the same Church that came into existence
on the Day of Pentecost. What applied to the Church at Jerusalem still
applies to the Church at Fort Worth—or wherever you live.) This event
in Acts occurred after the Resurrection and the enduement of power on
the Day of Pentecost. Jesus was already sitting at the right hand of the
Father where He sits today. Nothing had changed. The people in the
multitudes were still being healed. The same power of the Holy Spirit
was still being manifest:

> And by the hands of the apostles were many signs and
> wonders wrought among the people; (and they were
> all with one accord in Solomon's porch. And of the rest
> durst no man join himself to them: but the people mag-
> nified them. And believers were the more added to The
> LORD, multitudes both of men and women.) Insomuch
> that they brought forth the sick into the streets, and laid
> them on beds and couches, that at the least the shadow
> of Peter passing by might overshadow some of them.
> There came also a multitude out of the cities round
> about unto Jerusalem, bringing sick folks, and them
> which were vexed with unclean spirits: and they were
> healed every one (Acts 5:12-16).

Jesus never told anyone they should keep their disease because God was trying to teach them something through it. Not one in all the vast throngs and multitudes was told that God wanted him to stay sick in order to give God glory. No, the Scripture tells us that *healing* brings glory to God—not sickness. The people glorified the God of Israel when they saw the dumb speak, the maimed made whole, the lame walking and the blind seeing (Matthew 15:31).

Never did anyone come to Jesus for healing and hear, "It is not God's will to heal you," for an answer.

"And, behold, there came a leper and worshipped him, saying, LORD, if thou wilt, thou canst make me clean. And Jesus put forth his hand, and touched him, saying, I will; be thou clean. And immediately his leprosy was cleansed" (Matthew 8:2-3).

Jesus straightened out the leper's theology in just two words: "I will." Healing is God's will, or Jesus would not have healed all who came to Him.

We also know that with God there is no breach nor deviation—no change. He is no respecter of persons (Acts 10:34). The ministry of Jesus is evidence of that.

The Bible teaches us that a good tree can only bear good fruit. Jesus said that a good tree cannot bear evil fruit (Matthew 7:18).

God is good. He could not be the source of any sickness. It is an abomination to His nature of love for people to believe that God made them sick.

There are those who say they know God does not make people sick, but they believe He does allow Satan to put sickness on them to teach them or to get them into His will.

God does not have to allow Satan to do evil. Satan is quick to bring disease to Christians *if they will allow it.* They must govern Satan in their lives and circumstances.

If you are not walking in God's WORD, you have no defense against Satan and his fruit of sickness. Your lack of knowledge of God's

WORD or lack of diligence to act on The WORD allows disease to fill your body.

God is never the source of sickness.

"Every good gift and every perfect gift is from above, and cometh down from the Father of lights,

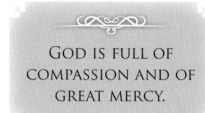

GOD IS FULL OF COMPASSION AND OF GREAT MERCY.

with whom is no variableness, neither shadow of turning" (James 1:17).

The Amplified Bible says there can be no variation in Him. This is a key to knowing the source of everything that comes your way in life. According to Scripture, we can say without reserve, every good gift is from above. Jesus came that we might have life.

Every evil, corrupt fruit is from Satan. He comes to steal, kill and destroy. Anything that brings doubt, discouragement or defeat is from him—*not from the Father.*

FAITH IN GOD'S MERCY

Many Christians today have the same attitude as the leper. They believe that God *can* heal, but they doubt that He *will* heal them. They believe in His ability, but not His mercy. They have no faith in God's love and mercy toward His family because they have no knowledge of His WORD.

When speaking to the Syrophoenician woman, Jesus called deliverance "the children's bread." If my children were hungry and knew I had bread, but didn't believe I would give it to them, all my care, love and affection would be in vain. I would rather they believe I *couldn't* give them what they needed than to believe that I *wouldn't*. I would much rather they doubted my ability than my love.

Theology teaches man about God's power, but for the most part, denies His willingness to use His power on man's behalf. Theology lacks the vital experience of the father-son relationship we can enjoy in Jesus as children of God. Man's idea of God always comes up short and lifeless. The mind of man is not capable of grasping that God is love unless it is revealed to him by God's Spirit through His WORD.

It is God's words about Himself on which we must base our faith. It would be foolish to believe what man (who has never even seen Him) says about God, rather than to believe what He says about Himself.

When Moses was alone with The LORD on Mount Sinai, he cried out to Him to see His glory. "And The LORD descended in the cloud, and stood with him there, and proclaimed the name of The LORD. And The LORD passed by before him, and proclaimed, The LORD, The LORD God, merciful and gracious, longsuffering, and abundant in goodness and truth" (Exodus 34:5-6).

God says of Himself that He is merciful and gracious, longsuffering (slow to anger), and abundant in goodness and truth.

The Bible magnifies God's mercy—His willingness to use His power to meet every need of man. The Scripture speaks of the "...exceeding greatness of his power to us-ward who believe" (Ephesians 1:19). His power is directed toward you, not away from you.

Psalm 145:8 says, "The LORD is gracious, and full of compassion; slow to anger, and of great mercy."

God is full of compassion and of great mercy. Mercy and compassion are translated from the same Greek word.

Compassion is a "moving or a yearning desire in the inward parts, the heart or spirit, toward another."[7] Compassion abides in the heart.

Jesus, in His high priestly ministry at the right hand of the Father, is moved with compassion or "touched" by our needs. "For we have not an high priest which cannot be touched with the feeling of our infirmities" (Hebrews 4:15). He is moved with compassion toward us.

Time after time, we see Jesus during His earthly ministry being moved

---

7   Vine, W.E., *An Expository Dictionary of Biblical Words*, (Old Tappan, N.J: Fleming H. Revell Company, 1966) Vol. I, p. 218.

with compassion and healing the sick. Compassion moved Him to extend to sufferers God's hand of mercy. It was the Father's compassion moving within Him. (Remember, He said He did nothing of Himself.) Because of His compassion, God's heart *yearns* to meet the needs of man.

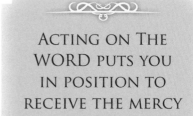

ACTING ON THE WORD PUTS YOU IN POSITION TO RECEIVE THE MERCY OF GOD.

One who does not know the Scriptures might wonder why, then, God does not heal all those who are sick, regardless of their position of faith. God's mercy goes forth in accordance with His covenant, The WORD. Because He has bound Himself by His WORD, He can move freely only toward those who are in a position to receive.

Acting on The WORD puts you in position to receive the mercy of God.

Mercy is God's attitude toward you in bestowing freely whatever is necessary to meet your needs. It manifests itself in actions and assumes the adequate resources to effect the proper result.[8]

It seems that mercy is the result of compassion. The inward moving of compassion results in the outward manifestation necessary to meet the need.

It is said of God in His WORD that He "delighteth in mercy" (Micah 7:18). The Bible speaks of "the tender mercy of our God" (Luke 1:78) and His "great mercy" (Numbers 14:18).

With your spirit, dare to stretch your faith to take in the boundless mercy of God.

You are the object of His mercy!

"O give thanks unto The LORD; for he is good: for his mercy endureth for ever" (Psalm 136:1).

"Know therefore that The LORD thy God, he is God, the faithful

---

8   Vine, W.E. (1966 edition), Vol. III, p. 60.

God, which keepeth covenant and mercy with them that love him and keep his commandments to a thousand generations" (Deuteronomy 7:9).

"For thou, LORD, art good, and ready to forgive; and plenteous in mercy unto all them that call upon thee" (Psalm 86:5).

His mercy endures forever! His willingness to act on man's behalf is still operating in the earth. It never runs out. It has never abated nor weakened.

He continues to keep mercy with them that love Him and do His WORD. And He is faithful to keep His covenant and offer His mercy.

It has been thousands of years since The LORD said His mercy extended to a thousand generations. It continues to reach you, day after day. He is still plenteous in mercy to them that call upon Him.

Praise The LORD! His mercy endureth forever! Mighty and powerful things happened when Israel said these words. They are words of praise and adoration to God.

When Solomon finished building the house of The LORD, the trumpeters and singers lifted their voices as one, and with trumpets, cymbals and instruments of music, they praised The LORD saying, "For he is good; for his mercy endureth for ever."

The glory of God filled the house so that the priests could not even minister because of the cloud (2 Chronicles 5:13-14). God Himself inhabited the praises of His people.

Jehoshaphat appointed singers to The LORD to go before the army and say, "Praise The LORD; for His mercy endureth for ever." As the Israelites began to sing and praise, The LORD set ambushments against their enemies, and they destroyed themselves (2 Chronicles 20:21-23).

The weapon of praise! Singers going before an army? It happened just that way. Israel never had to unsheathe a weapon of war—only to sing "Praise The LORD. For His mercy endureth forever."

SPEAK OF HIS COMPASSION AND MERCY

It brings honor to the Father when we believe His WORD and magnify His love and mercy. We honor and praise Him when we speak of His goodness and lovingkindness.

It honors Him when we speak of Him as our Father of love who does only good. Speak of the great God of the universe who is eager to BLESS and who even gave His own Son because He so loved the world.

Speak of The LORD whose eyes "...run to and fro throughout the whole earth to show Himself strong in behalf of those whose heart is blameless toward Him" (2 Chronicles 16:9, *The Amplified Bible*).

When you speak of Him in this manner, you are praising Him. We are told to continually offer up to Him a sacrifice of praise (Hebrews 13:15).

David was a man after God's own heart who knew how to praise his God. Until you have The WORD dwelling in you richly so that you can speak psalms and praises out of your own spirit, use the praises of David to magnify God. Speak them or sing them out loud to the Father.

Here is Psalm 9:1-4:

> I will praise thee, O LORD, with my whole heart; I will
> show forth all thy marvellous works. I will be glad and
> rejoice in thee: I will sing praise to thy name, O thou
> most High. When mine enemies are turned back, they
> shall fall and perish at thy presence. For thou hast main-
> tained my right and my cause; thou satest in the throne
> judging right.

The WORD says that God inhabits the praises of His people (Psalm 22:3). The enemy is turned back, falls and perishes at the presence of our God.

Praise not only honors God and empowers our faith, but it also is

> IT HONORS HIM WHEN WE SPEAK OF HIM AS OUR FATHER OF LOVE WHO DOES ONLY GOOD.

a powerful weapon where Satan is concerned. When we praise God, it works deliverance for us.

Abraham "...grew strong and was empowered by faith as he gave praise and glory to God" (Romans 4:20, *The Amplified Bible*). As you praise God and speak of His marvelous works, faith rises on the inside of you to receive THE BLESSING of God.

Honor God with your words, bringing them into agreement with God's words about Him. Look in His WORD for good things to proclaim about Him. As you publish The LORD's mercy and compassion to those around you, tell others of the great things He has done in your life.

Refuse to allow *your* words to be an affront to the Father God and His nature of love. It is a matter of your will. Notice that David says, "I *will* praise, I *will* show forth thy marvellous works, I *will* be glad and rejoice, I *will* sing praise." You do not just praise God because you feel like it. You praise Him because you will to praise Him.

Say with David, "I will praise thee, O LORD, with my whole heart...."

Great things happen when you continually confess the mercy of God. Faith rises up on the inside of you and *the reality that God loves you* begins to sing through your spirit!

When God's mercy first became a reality to me, it was so alive in my heart that I continually confessed, "Praise The LORD. His mercy endureth forever!" Something supernatural happened inside me. My faith rose to the knowledge of God's mercy and that it continually surrounded me.

Psalm 118:4 admonishes us to confess God's mercy: "Let them now that fear The LORD say, that his mercy endureth for ever."

Put these words constantly on your lips. (For an example, look at Psalm 136.) You will begin to experience the thrill and the joy of realizing that God is indeed "rich in mercy" because of His great love with which He loves us (Ephesians 2:4).

GREAT THINGS HAPPEN WHEN YOU CONTINUALLY CONFESS THE MERCY OF GOD.

As you confess God's mercy, you will expect and say, "Surely goodness and mercy shall follow me all the days of my life." You will realize that mercy is continually coming out of the heart of God and that His mercy is new every morning (Lamentations 3:22-23).

"Let us therefore come boldly unto the throne of grace, that we may obtain mercy, and find grace to help in time of need" (Hebrews 4:16).

Because of God's WORD and what you have read, your faith has risen where God's mercy is concerned. You are now in position to come boldly to the throne of grace and obtain mercy and find grace to help in time of need!

GOD'S MEDICINE

Proverbs 4:20-23 says, "My son, attend to my words; incline thine ear unto my sayings. Let them not depart from thine eyes; keep them in the midst of thine heart. For they are life unto those that find them, and health to all their flesh. Keep thy heart with all diligence; for out of it are the issues of life." This is God's prescription for life and health!

"Attend to my words." Give your undivided attention to God's WORD, and pay heed to what He says. If you attend to someone, you take care of that person. Give your time, thought and meditation to The WORD. Give action to it. Continually give it first place in your life.

The result? "Thou wilt keep him in perfect peace, whose mind is stayed on thee: because he trusteth in thee" (Isaiah 26:3). And, your mind will be free from doubt when you keep your attention on God's WORD because when you are trusting in God's WORD, you are trusting in Him. So, stay your mind on The WORD. Because you are committing yourself to it, fear and doubt will be driven out, and it *will* keep you in perfect peace.

Check your peace level. If you are not enjoying peace, you are not staying your mind on Him!

"Incline thine ears." Open your understanding to take in God's sayings. Desire and go after the knowledge of His WORD. Put your physical ears in position to hear the word of faith preached. Take your ears to places where The WORD is going forth and listen to audio resources about The WORD. They are such wonderful and valuable tools to get The WORD into your heart. Faith comes by hearing the preached WORD of God. So, listen to what is being said with your spiritual ears.

Jesus said:

> If any man has ears to hear, let him be listening and perceive and comprehend. And He said to them, Be careful what you are hearing. The measure [of thought and study] you give [to the truth you hear] will be the measure [of virtue and knowledge] that comes back to you—and more [besides] will be given to you who hear. For to him who has will more be given; and from him who has nothing, even what he has will be taken away (by force) (Mark 4:23-25, *The Amplified Bible*).

Every man to whom Jesus was speaking that day had physical ears. Jesus was referring to receiving God's WORD in the heart by listening to the Holy Spirit speak revelation knowledge. Listen with your spiritual ears as well as your physical ears.

Jesus was not just talking about passively hearing, either. He said listen, perceive and comprehend, and even be careful *how* you hear. The time you give to digesting The WORD you hear will measure the return of the virtue (power) and knowledge that will come back to you through that WORD.

The man who hears (or receives revelation knowledge) will be given more. If you want to grow in the knowledge of God, be careful *how* you hear His WORD.

"Let them not depart from thine eyes." Keep your eyes trained on God's WORD. Do not look at circumstances or feelings that appear contrary to your healing. Look at God's WORD. Give attention to what He says. Consider (or give thought to) it instead of your body. Keep it ever before your eyes. Jesus said, "The light of the body is the eye: if therefore thine eye be single, thy whole body shall be full of light" (Matthew 6:22).

This scripture reveals why it is so important that we do not let The WORD depart from our sight. The eye is the gateway to the body.

If your eye or your attention is on the darkness—the sickness—in your body, there will be no light to expel that darkness. Your eye is unsound, therefore, your body is, and will continue to be, unsound. But, cause your eye to become single on The WORD of God, and your whole body will be full of light. The single eye allows no darkness to enter.

What you do with your eyes in some cases is a matter of life and death. To look at sickness brings death. To look at God's WORD brings life.

"Keep them in the midst of thine heart." Allow God's WORD to abide in you by meditating and acting on what you hear. The portion of God's WORD you act on is the portion of His WORD living in you. Continually feed yourself with The WORD to keep it producing the force of faith. Inclining your ear and refusing to allow it to depart from your eyes keeps it alive in your heart.

"For they are life unto those that find them, and health to all their flesh." God's sayings are life. Jesus said, "[My words] are spirit, and they are

life" (John 6:63). They are life to whom? They are life to those that find them and *health to all their flesh* (Proverbs 4:22). God's words are life and health. They are His medicine.

Continually attending to The WORD with your ears, your eyes and your heart will cause you to live in divine health. It will be as hard for you to get sick as it was once difficult for you to be healed because the power of The WORD is continually being made life and health to your body.

By doing these things diligently, you are keeping your heart. "Keep thy heart with all diligence; for out of it are the issues of life" (verse 23). From the midst of your heart are continually coming the forces (issues) of life, bringing healing and health to your flesh. *The WORD in your heart produces life and health in your body.*

Several times since I have learned to walk in faith, almost before I realized it, I became too sick to stay on my feet. (I have learned since then to go to The WORD at the first sign of a symptom—I immediately take a dose of God's medicine!)

I turn to 1 Peter 2:24, read it aloud, and receive my healing. I play the New Testament on tape and listen to The WORD. Usually, I go to sleep listening to it. Either the next morning or in a few hours, I awaken, completely healed. God's medicine effects a healing and a cure in my body.

To be sick and receive healing is not God's best. To receive healing is wonderful, but to live in divine health is better. Ken and I have learned to believe in divine health, not just in healing. We endeavor to maintain our health by The WORD and not allow sickness to obtain a foothold.

To fill God's prescription for life and health, you must be diligent to attend to His WORD. You must give it the place of authority and spend time in it *daily*. The forces of life and power coming out of your heart will be in direct proportion to the amount of The WORD that goes in you.

There is no limit to the amount of God's medicine you can take. You cannot get an overdose. The more you take, the more powerful you become!

HE BORE OUR SICKNESSES

"That it might be fulfilled which was spoken by Esaias the prophet, saying, Himself took our infirmities, and bare our sicknesses" (Matthew 8:17).

When Jesus bore away our sins, He also bore away our diseases. The Cross pronounced a double cure for the ills of mankind. The Church of Jesus Christ has been made just as free from sickness as it has been made free from sin. A Christian may continue to sin after he has been born again, but he doesn't have to. Sin can no longer lord it over him unless he allows it (Romans 6:14).

A Christian may continue to be sick after he has been born again *but he doesn't have to.* He has been redeemed from sickness. The price has been paid for his healing. Sickness can no longer exert dominion over him unless *he* allows it.

Most believers have only known a part of their redemption. Their faith will operate to the degree of their knowledge of God's WORD. They would have begun to live in divine health long ago had they realized that healing belonged to them.

As you accept the fact that as surely as Jesus bore your sins, He also bore away your diseases, weakness and pain, your days of sickness will be over.

The light of God's WORD will also destroy Satan's grip on your life in the area of physical suffering. The truth makes you free from his dominion when you realize that your healing has been purchased by the sacrifice of Jesus.

Isaiah 53:4-5 says, "Surely he hath borne our griefs, and carried our sorrows: yet we did esteem him stricken, smitten of God, and afflicted. But he was wounded for our transgressions, he was bruised for our iniquities: the chastisement of our peace was upon him; and with his stripes we are healed." This whole chapter is all about Jesus being made the substitute for man. It says, "Surely he hath borne our griefs." *Young's*

Analytical Concordance to the Bible[9] says *choli,* translated *griefs,* means "sickness, weakness and pain."

Surely (Hebrew: truly, certainly, firmly) He has borne your sickness, weakness and pain! Allow yourself to receive the magnitude of what God is speaking to you.

Jesus was smitten of God with sin and sickness in order for you to go free. Verse 6 tells us, "The LORD hath laid on him the iniquity of us all." Verse 10: "Yet it pleased The LORD to bruise him; he hath put him to grief." (According to Dr. Young the word *grief* means "to make sick" and should be translated, "He has made Him sick.")

According to God's WORD, what did Jesus do with your sickness? He bore it for you. So, it could not be God's will for you to be sick with the sickness that Jesus already suffered for you.

Because God so loved the world, He engineered the substitution of His only begotten Son to redeem man from the curse of the law:

> Christ hath redeemed us from the curse of the law, being
> made a curse for us: for it is written, Cursed is every one
> that hangeth on a tree (Galatians 3:13).

Jesus was willing to take the curse in His own spirit, soul and body so that you would not have to continue under Satan's dominion.

There was no sickness before man became one with Satan. Sin is the root from which sickness came. *Just as sin is the manifestation of spiritual death in the heart of man, sickness is the manifestation of spiritual death in the body of man.*

Jesus came to destroy the works of the devil—*all* his works (1 John 3:8). He did not destroy sin only to leave sickness in dominion. Partial redemption from Satan's power would not have pleased God, nor

---

9   Robert Young, *Young's Analytical Concordance to the Bible* (Peabody, MA: Hendrickson Publishers) "Grief"

would it have fulfilled His plan for His family.

God redeemed the whole man: righteousness for his nature, peace for his mind and healing for his body. Redemption left nothing in force that came on man because of sin. Jesus completely destroyed the works of the devil in the lives of men.

> For ye are bought with a price: therefore glorify God
> in your body, and in your spirit, which are God's
> (1 Corinthians 6:20).

> And thus He fulfilled what was spoken by the prophet
> Isaiah, He Himself took [in order to carry away] our
> weaknesses and infirmities and bore away our diseases
> (Matthew 8:17, *The Amplified Bible*).

> Who his own self bare our sins in his own body
> on the tree, that we, being dead to sins, should live
> unto righteousness: by whose stripes ye were healed
> (1 Peter 2:24).

"By whose stripes ye were healed" is not a promise. *It is a fact.* It has already taken place. Jesus bore sickness away from you, and by His stripes you *were* healed. Hebrews 4:12 says, "For The WORD that God speaks is alive and full of power—[making it active, operative, energizing and effective]" *(The Amplified Bible).*

The words spoken out of the mouth of God are forever settled in heaven. When He has said it once, He has said it forever. His words never die nor lose their power. In Genesis 1:14 it says, "And God said, Let there be lights in the firmament of the heaven to divide the day from the night." God does not have to get up every morning about 4 o'clock and command the sun to rise and shine! The WORD He spoke at Creation is still alive and full of power, enforcing the result for which it was sent.

Throughout the reaches of time, the words God spoke that day continue to operate the sun, moon and stars in their function of giving light to the earth. Because of His mighty words, "Let there be lights in the firmament," they would not dare cease to give forth. His command is still in effect, and will be, until He changes it.

His WORD has gone forth out of His mouth concerning your healing and it is still in effect. Men cannot change it. Many have tried, even saying that healing has passed away. *But God says* that Jesus bore our sicknesses and carried our diseases, and by His stripes we were healed.

God's WORD is alive! He watches over it to perform it and His presence is ever over His WORD to bring it to pass. It is His WORD to you now. His WORD about healing has the power in it to accomplish the purpose for which it is sent—the healing of your body. It is just the same as if Jesus called you by your name and said, "I bore your sicknesses and carried your diseases, and by My stripes you are healed."

When you have seen it in The WORD—you have heard from God! Your healing would be no more valid and sure if Jesus appeared to you in person and spoke these words.

Meditate on and confess these scriptures until the reality of your healing literally dominates your mind and body.

ACCEPT JESUS AS HEALER

Make the decision to live in divine health in the same way you made the decision to accept Jesus as Savior. Decide to be well!

Just as salvation is being offered to whosoever will, healing is being offered to whosoever will.

The Greek word *sozo,* translated *saved* in Romans 10:9, is the same Greek word translated *healed* in the Gospels. In Mark 5:23 Jairus said to Jesus, "I pray thee, come and lay thy hands on her, that she may be healed *(sozo)*; and she shall live." To the woman with the issue of blood

Jesus said, "Daughter, be of good comfort; thy faith hath made thee whole *(sozo)"* (Matthew 9:22).

When Jesus was raised from the dead, He purchased soundness for your spirit, soul and body. You have been made whole.

Right now, by faith, confess Jesus as your healer in the same way you made Him LORD over your life. Make Jesus LORD over your body according to Romans 10:10:

WHEN JESUS WAS RAISED FROM THE DEAD, HE PURCHASED SOUNDNESS FOR YOUR SPIRIT, SOUL AND BODY.

> According to The WORD of God, I confess with my mouth that Jesus is LORD. I confess Him as my healer. I make Him LORD over my body. I believe in my heart that God raised Him from the dead. From this moment, my body is saved, healed, made whole and delivered.

Resist the temptation to be sick just as you resist temptation to sin. That may sound too simple, but it works because The WORD says, "Resist the devil, and he will flee from you" (James 4:7).

Satan is the source of sickness. When he attempts to put sickness on your body, refuse it in the Name of Jesus!

It is against the will of God for you to be sick.

As soon as you have even the slightest indication that Satan is tempting you with sickness, turn to 1 Peter 2:24 and read it aloud. Receive it in faith and thank God that by His stripes you were healed.

You *will* have an opportunity to "stand fast therefore in the liberty wherewith Christ hath made us free" because the devil will try to talk you out of your healing. But, the price has already been paid for you to be healed. With Jesus as your Healer, the power of His Name, His WORD and His Spirit, you can enjoy, not only divine healing, but divine health.

BELIEVE YOU RECEIVE

To get results, you must believe you receive your healing *when you pray*—not after you are well.

You are to join Abraham and consider not your own body, but only what God says (Romans 4:20). The symptoms of sickness may continue to linger after you believe you receive, but this is the time you must hold fast to a fearless confession of The WORD.

Hebrews 10:35-36 says, "Do not, therefore, fling away your fearless confidence, for it carries a great and glorious compensation of reward. For you have need of steadfast patience and endurance, so that you may perform and fully accomplish the will of God, and thus receive and carry away [and enjoy to the full] what is promised" *(The Amplified Bible)*.

Do not allow your fearless confidence in God's WORD to be snatched away from you by Satan. You must walk by faith and not by sight.

E.W. Kenyon teaches that there are three witnesses in receiving healing: The WORD, the pain or sickness, and you.[10] You are the deciding factor. If you join your confession with the pain, you are crossing The WORD that says you are healed. If you align your confession with God's WORD, you will have to cross the pain. The Bible teaches that by two witnesses a thing is established. *You* make the choice. Agree with the pain, and sickness will rule. Dare to agree with The WORD, and healing will be established. The circumstances will follow your action and confession.

Know that God's WORD does not fail. Steadfastly and patiently refuse to be moved by what you see. The WORD will change what you can see. Be moved by The WORD and by your confession of Jesus as healer.

Satan tried to tell you that you were not saved. He comes to the

---

10 E.W. Kenyon, *The Two Kinds of Knowledge* (Los Angeles: Kenyon Gospel Publishing Society, 2000) chapter 9, p. 40

new Christian with doubts about
salvation. Now, his symptoms of
pain or fever are trying to convince you that you are not healed.
Stand fast in the knowledge of
God's WORD.

> DO NOT ALLOW
> YOUR FEARLESS
> CONFIDENCE IN
> GOD'S WORD TO
> BE SNATCHED AWAY
> FROM YOU.

Jesus told the nobleman, "Thy
son liveth," and the boy *began* to
amend *from that hour.*

When you believe you receive
healing, you may be healed instantly or you may have to act on your
covenant of healing, even though your body does not feel healed. But
one thing is certain: When you believe you receive, healing begins to take
place in your body. God is a covenant-keeping God. He could not keep
His covenant without healing you, if you have met the conditions of that
covenant.

You are learning to be moved by The WORD of God instead of by
what you feel or see. This is how faith operates. You are becoming that
faith man or woman you have yearned to be.

As you use your faith to act on God's WORD it becomes stronger,
and as you learn to stand against Satan and his symptoms, it becomes
easier. But there is no formula that will work effectively unless you continually exert the force of faith through feeding on The WORD.

If you will continually feed on God's WORD, you will come to the
place where you simply go to 1 Peter 2:24 and enforce The WORD that
you *were* healed, thank God for His WORD of healing, and then go on
about your business.

When I revised this book, many years after I wrote the original
manuscript, I wanted to include these healing scriptures and to show you
how I use them when necessary.

John and Dodie Osteen, personal friends of ours, as well as parents of

Joel Osteen, pastored Lakewood Church in Houston, Texas, until 1999, when John went home to be with The LORD. While they were pastoring the church, Dodie was diagnosed with terminal liver cancer. The doctor told John and Dodie that medical science could not cure her, so they decided to go home from the hospital.

Dodie began to take God's WORD just as you would take medicine prescribed by a doctor. For several years, she saturated herself with God's WORD concerning healing.

There are specific scriptures she "took," like medicine, into her mind, heart and body every day, without fail, regardless of what was happening around her. Today, she is totally cured of terminal cancer and has been for many years. However, she continues taking God's medicine, daily, to keep The WORD concerning her healing before her eyes and in her heart.

The following scriptures, for the most part, are taken from the scriptures she uses. I've added some as I've taken them for the healing of my own body. Take this list and add any other healing and faith-building scriptures that minister to you. When you are standing for healing, don't let a day go by without receiving His WORD into yourself. Do it more than once a day if the situation is severe. I say them out loud so that I both see and hear the words—that's how The WORD gets into your heart! You can also take this medicine when you are well to stay well.

Exodus 15:26	Mark 11:23-24
Exodus 23:25	Mark 16:17-18
Deuteronomy 7:15	John 10:10
Deuteronomy 28:1-14, 61	Romans 4:17-21
Deuteronomy 30:19-20	Romans 8:11
Joshua 21:45	2 Corinthians 10:3-6

1 Kings 8:56	Galatians 3:13
Psalm 91:15-16	Ephesians 6:10-17
Psalm 103:2-6	Philippians 1:6
Psalm 107:20-21	Philippians 2:13-14
Proverbs 4:20-24	Hebrews 10:23
Isaiah 40:29-31	Hebrews 10:35-38
Isaiah 41:10	Hebrews 11:1, 11
Isaiah 53:4-5	Hebrews 13:8
Jeremiah 1:12	James 5:14-15
Jeremiah 30:17a	1 Peter 2:24
Matthew 8:16b-17	1 John 5:14-15
Matthew 18:18-19	Revelation 12:11
Matthew 21:21	

SCRIPTURE:

"And Jesus, moved with compassion, put forth his hand, and touched him, and saith unto him, I will: be thou clean" (Mark 1:41).

Points to Remember:

1. You have a covenant with God that includes divine health. Believe you receive *when you pray* and *before you see* because God's WORD says the answer belongs to you. And according to Jesus, you shall have what you desire from the Father.

2. If you will continually feed on God's WORD, you will come to the place where you simply go to 1 Peter 2:24 and enforce The WORD that you *were* healed, thank God for His WORD of healing, and then go on about your business.

Confession:

I believe that Jesus is LORD, and that He was raised from the dead for me. I believe He purchased my redemption. That redemption includes divine healing and health. Therefore, I confess Jesus as my healer. I make Him LORD over my body. I believe in my heart that God raised Him from the dead. From this moment, my body is saved, healed, made whole and delivered.

The incorruptible seed of The WORD of God is working mightily in me. I believe 1 Peter 2:24, and when symptoms come against my body, I stand on God's mighty WORD, that "by his stripes ye *were* healed." I refuse to allow symptoms to stay in my body. Jesus bore my sicknesses and diseases. Because He already paid the price on the Cross, I am redeemed from every curse of the law and completely healed and whole—now and forever!

CHAPTER FIVE

God's Will Is Love

I t is God's will that His love be the distinguishing mark of every be-
liever. The world does not see the love between the believer and the
Father as much as it sees the love between the believer and his brother.
You have been given the love of God with which to love one another.

The character of natural man is selfish. But, when you are born again,
that selfishness is replaced by the love of God. "This new kind of love is
the nature of God, imparted to man in the new birth." [11]

Only the Father and His children have the ability to operate in
this kind of love. It is the God-kind of love translated from the Greek
word *agape*. This word for love is only used in connection with the
family of God.

Second Timothy 1:7 says, "For God hath not given us the spirit of
fear; but of power, and of love, and of a sound mind." God has given
us the Spirit of love. And, Romans 5:5 says, "...the love of God is shed
abroad in our hearts by the Holy Ghost which is given unto us."

---

11 Kenyon, E.W., *The Hidden Man* (Lynnwood, Wash.: Kenyon's Gospel Publishing
Society, 1998) p. 22.

First John 4:8 tells us, "He that loveth not knoweth not God; for God is love." This God-kind of love is not what you do but what you are.

In Ephesians 4:24, the Apostle Paul says we are to "put on the new man, which after God is created in righteousness and true holiness." God is love, and you have been re-

GOD IS LOVE, AND YOU HAVE BEEN RE-CREATED IN HIS IMAGE.... *YOU ARE THE LOVE OF GOD.*

created in His image. Your new nature is *agape* love. *You are the love of God.*

What a privilege that God would make us His love! No wonder Jesus said that all men would know us by this new kind of love. This love had never been manifest to the world before Jesus came in the flesh and walked among men.

The world is starved for love. God made man to receive love. The deepest yearning of every man is to be loved and cared for—a desire that can only be totally fulfilled through the love of God. The world today will never see the love of God until believers learn to walk in the fullness of this powerful force. This love starvation is a major reason for mental breakdown, physical sickness and the ills of mankind. People without love are unhappy and can find no ease for this inborn hunger. (No ease brings *dis*ease.)

Everyone on the face of the earth should experience the love of God. What an honor the Father has bestowed upon you—the ability and the right to love and be loved *with His love.* You are the open door into the love of God for the people with whom you come in contact.

The new commandment of love was given to you personally by Jesus: "That ye love one another, as I have loved you" (John 15:12). We have been commanded to love as Jesus loved. "As the Father hath loved me, so have I loved you: continue ye in my love" (John 15:9). Jesus loved as the Father loved. Now, *we* are to love as He loved.

If it were not possible for you to obey this commandment, God would not have given it. It is the law of the new creature. "Love worketh no ill to *his* neighbour: therefore love is the fulfilling of the law" (Romans 13:10). Love fulfills all the law. Notice, this verse says, "Love worketh no ill to *his* neighbour." Not, "its" neighbor. The believer works no ill to *his* neighbor. The believer *is* love. When you obey the love law of the family of God, you are performing God's perfect will in your life!

"Faith begins where the will of God is known."[12] As you learn about this God-kind of love from The WORD, the force of faith will rise up in you to live the love life. The world's idea of love does not compare with this *agape* love. It is a poor counterfeit for God's love. *Agape* is beyond human understanding. You must learn from The WORD what love is and what God says concerning His love. Then, you can begin to reveal to the world the love that you have been made in Christ Jesus.

THIS IS LOVE

> For this is the love of God, that we keep his commandments: and his commandments are not grievous (1 John 5:3).

> And what this love consists in is this: that we live and walk in accordance with and guided by His commandments (His orders, ordinances, precepts, teaching). This is the commandment, as you have heard from the beginning, that you continue to walk in love [guided by it and following it] (2 John 6, *The Amplified Bible*).

God defines His love as keeping His commandments—walking after His teaching. This brings love out of the indefinite into something clearly

---

12 F.F. Bosworth, *Christ the Healer* (Grand Rapids: Fleming H. Revell, 1973) p. 40.

defined, so you can know how to love as He loves. God has given us His love manual written in black and white! Obeying His WORD is walking in His love.

If you are born again, you are the love of God by nature. Faith is born into you when you are begotten of God. But, until you begin to act on His WORD, that powerful force lies dormant. The same is true concerning the love of God. You can have the love of God abiding within you and yet be unable to allow it to work through you to reach others. Without revelation knowledge, love lies undeveloped, and selfishness continues to reign in the new creature. Faith and love become active through knowledge of The WORD. The Apostle Paul said in Philippians 1:9, "And this I pray, that your love may abound yet more and more in knowledge and in all judgment."

PERFECTED LOVE

"But whoso keepeth his WORD, in him verily is the love of God perfected: hereby know we that we are in him. He that saith he abideth in him ought himself also so to walk, even as he walked" (1 John 2:5-6).

As you act on God's WORD, the love of God is perfected in you. Through His WORD, the Holy Spirit manifests the love nature of the Father in you, and as you continue to adhere to the message of love, it will flow from you to others.

God's love is not being what the world considers "sweet." It is obeying Love Himself by obeying the teaching of His WORD.

How accurately you perfect the love walk will measure how much of the perfect will of God you accomplish. The Bible teaches us that faith works by love. Answered prayer is almost impossible when a believer refuses to forgive or is in strife.

The beginning of 1 Corinthians 13, the love chapter, says the gifts of the Spirit are nothing without love. Tongues are just noise if there is no love. If a person has the gift of prophecy, understands all knowledge and has enough faith to move mountains, without love he is nothing. If he gives all that he has to the poor and even sacrifices his life, without the love of God, he gains nothing.

Without love, your giving will not work. Tongues and prophecy will not work, faith fails and knowledge is unfruitful. All the truths you have learned from God's WORD work by love. They will profit you little unless you live the love of God.

AGAPE LOVE

Love endures long and is patient and kind; love never is envious nor boils over with jealousy; is not boastful or vainglorious, does not display itself haughtily. It is not conceited (arrogant and inflated with pride); it is not rude (unmannerly) and does not act unbecomingly. Love (God's love in us) does not insist on its own rights or its own way, for it is not self-seeking; it is not touchy or fretful or resentful; it takes no account of the evil done to it [it pays no attention to a suffered wrong]. It does not rejoice at injustice and unrighteousness, but rejoices when right and truth prevail. Love bears up under anything and everything that comes, is ever ready to believe the best of every person, its hopes are fadeless under all circumstances, and it endures everything [without weakening]. Love never fails [never fades out or becomes obsolete or comes to an end] (1 Corinthians 13:4-8, *The Amplified Bible*).

You are a love creature, and you *can* live the love life. God not only re-created your spirit in the image of love, but He also sent His love Spirit to live in you and teach you how to love as He loves.

Become love conscious by confessing and acting on God's WORD concerning this love. As you meditate on these scriptures, see yourself living the love life. Read these scriptures aloud with yourself in love's place:

> I endure long, and I am patient and kind. I am never envious nor do I boil over with jealousy. I am not boastful or vainglorious and I do not display myself haughtily. I am not conceited—arrogant and inflated with pride. I am not rude (unmannerly), and I do not act unbecomingly. I do not insist on my own rights or my own way because I am not self-seeking. I am not touchy, fretful or resentful. I take no account of the evil done to me—I pay no attention to a suffered wrong. I do not rejoice at injustice and unrighteousness, but I rejoice when right and truth prevail. I bear up under anything and everything that comes, I am ever ready to believe the best of every person, my hopes are fadeless under all circumstances, and I endure everything without weakening. I never fail.

You must make the decision to perfect the love of God in your life. No one else can do it for you. Make the decision in faith and commit yourself to obey God's WORD about love. There will be times when you'd rather do anything than allow love to rule. (It will seem as though it is taking off a pound of flesh!) It would be much easier to go ahead and become angry, seek your own and retaliate. It is an area, as in healing, when you must demand that your senses (flesh) be subject to The WORD.

Without a definite decision, you will not continue in the love of God. Commit yourself to *agape,* and when temptation comes, you will remember this decision and obey love. Remember that everything else depends on it.

COMMIT YOURSELF
TO OBEY
GOD'S WORD
ABOUT LOVE.

After making the decision, the most powerful thing you can do in perfecting the love walk is to continually confess that you are the love of God by speaking 1 Corinthians 13:4-8. This God-kind of love will begin to influence all you say and do. If someone says something unkind to you, love will say, "That's OK. I am not touchy, fretful or resentful. I take no account of that"—and, you go free!

Proverbs 17:9 says, "He who covers and forgives an offense seeks love, but he who repeats or harps on a matter separates even close friends" *(The Amplified Bible)*. If you hear ugly gossip about your brother, love will say, "I do not rejoice at unrighteousness." Instead of telling everyone what you heard of the brother's transgression, the love of God in you will want to cover or hide it for his sake. You no longer rejoice at unrighteousness. You are committed to love, and love believes the best.

Love *never* fails. Nothing works without it, and there can be no failure with it. When you stay in love, you cannot fail.

Learn to believe in love. It is the most powerful force in the universe. Walk in love by faith in The WORD. Walking in love is walking in the spirit—walking as Jesus walked. It is directly opposed to the senses, which have been trained to put themselves and their desires above everything else. The natural man has been highly trained in the area of seeking his own—selfishness. But love does not seek its own rights or its own way. It takes the operation of faith to believe that love's way will not fail.

The natural mind cannot understand this love because natural men and their world are ruled by selfishness. The natural man believes, *"If I don't look out for No. 1* (himself), *no one else will."* He's right. No one else can. His selfishness just shut the door to the love of God that never fails.

When you practice love by faith and refuse to seek your own, you put the Father into action, who will allow no man to do you wrong. As long as you stay in love, God the Father seeks your own. He sees to it that love never fails. Walking in love is to your great advantage!

Agape love is a new kind of power. It makes you the master of every situation. As long as you walk in love, you cannot be hurt, nor can you fail. No weapon that is formed against you will prosper. No one even has the power to hurt your feelings because you are not ruled by feelings, but by God's love. You are loving as He loves.

You no longer seek your own, yet your success is guaranteed!

This love is revolutionary. If men knew the great return from living God's love, each would try to love the other more! E.W. Kenyon, in his book *The New Kind of Love,*[13] accurately tagged this *agape* love *a new kind of selfishness.* The more you love, the greater you are!

TWO SPIRITUAL KINGDOMS

Giving thanks unto the Father, which hath made us meet to be partakers of the inheritance of the saints in light: who hath delivered us from the power of darkness, and hath translated us into the kingdom of his dear Son: in whom we have redemption through his blood, even the forgiveness of sins (Colossians 1:12-14).

You have been delivered out of the kingdom of darkness and translated into the kingdom of His Son. You became a citizen of this Kingdom when you made Jesus LORD. You have been redeemed from Satan's authority.

There are two realms operating in the world today. They are spiritual kingdoms and must be spiritually discerned. Only the children of God

13 E.W. Kenyon, *The New Kind of Love* (Lynnwood, Wash.: Kenyon's Gospel Publishing Society, 1981).

can live in the kingdom of light. In the kingdom of darkness, Satan and his children dwell. They are bound to darkness until someone tells them about Jesus. It is also possible for Christians to be lured by the devil into operating in this spiritual darkness.

That darkness to which you were once bound no longer has any dominion or control over you unless you allow Satan to lure you back into it. For a Christian to walk or live in the darkness does not mean he has lost his redemption. It does mean that he is not enjoying his inheritance with the saints in the light. The inheritance is still his. It belongs to him, but he is not taking advantage of it.

Paul spoke to the Corinthians concerning living as mere men. You can continue to live the same old life after you have been born again, and you probably will, unless someone teaches you The WORD. You have to learn from The WORD of God what your redemption is before you can begin to live it. You must learn how to live in the light as He is in the light.

Have you read of people eating out of trash cans and begging, being found dead with thousands of dollars in their possession? They had the money to buy food, but refused to use it, and chose instead to live like animals.

You may choose to live as a mere man and continue to be ruled by the darkness of the world, identifying with your old life. You may choose to continue to be selfish, sick and not healed. You may live in want instead of abundance or continue to sin, live the low life, and believe only what you see, feel, touch, taste and hear. The choice is yours.

In the kingdom of darkness, Satan rules, and men are driven by selfishness. Their authority is sense knowledge—limited to what can be seen, felt, tasted, smelled or heard. This keeps them in darkness. They do not see God. They walk in darkness, which produces failure. Failure brings them lack and poverty. The fear in this darkness drives and torments them. Their lives hang in doubt—the assurance of life is not theirs to enjoy. This fear and doubt produce sickness in their bodies and minds. They are subject to the law of sin and death continually in operation in this kingdom.

Now, you are light. You are no longer darkness, nor are you bound to it. Ephesians 5:8 says, "For ye were sometimes darkness, but now are ye light in The LORD: walk as children of light." You have a choice. You can identify with the saints in light, walking as children of light—learning The WORD of God, living in divine health and prospering in all you do. *You can be love ruled.*

KEEP YOURSELF IN LOVE

"We know that whosoever is born of God sinneth not; but he that is begotten of God keepeth himself, and that wicked one toucheth him not" (1 John 5:18).

Would you like to be this man whom the wicked one cannot touch? This inheritance belongs to you. *You can keep yourself in light.*

Satan cannot touch you as long as you are walking in the light. He is darkness and cannot penetrate the kingdom of light. When you walk in light, in love, in The WORD and in fellowship, *the wicked one touches you not.*

These kingdoms are two distinct realms. A step out of love is a step into Satan's realm. There is no gray area between the light and the darkness. You are either walking in love—in light—or walking in enemy territory—in darkness.

The kingdom of light is the kingdom of God. The authority of the kingdom of light is The WORD of God, which produces love. This Kingdom is ruled by the love of God. When you walk in the spirit, you are operating in this Kingdom and controlling your affairs through guidance from the Holy Spirit of God. Therefore, you are continually walking in God's wisdom, which guarantees success in all you do.

When you operate in the kingdom of light, you are living by faith.

Joy and peace are ever in you. Your body lives in health, and the wisdom of God produces material abundance. The law of the Spirit of life in Christ Jesus continually works in this Kingdom.

To walk in God is to walk in the light. To walk in the light is to walk in The WORD. To walk in The WORD is to walk in love. To walk in love is to walk in the spirit. To walk in the spirit is to walk in wisdom. To walk in wisdom is to walk in success. And to walk in success is to walk in God.

Make your confession now: "I keep myself in the kingdom of light, in love and in The WORD, and the wicked one touches me not!"

Jesus says in Matthew 6:33 that we are to continually seek after this kingdom of light: "But seek ye first the kingdom of God, and his righteousness; and all these things shall be added unto you."

WALKING IN THE LIGHT

This then is the message which we have heard of him,
and declare unto you, that God is light, and in him is
no darkness at all. If we say that we have fellowship with
him, and walk in darkness, we lie, and do not the truth:
But if we walk in the light, as he is in the light, we have
fellowship one with another, and the blood of Jesus
Christ his Son cleanseth us from all sin (1 John 1:5-7).

The believer sins by breaking the new commandment *that ye love one another.* If you have fellowship with your brother, you are walking in the light as He is in the light, and you have fellowship with the Father.

God is love. God is light. Walking in Him is walking in love, in fellowship and in The WORD. Psalm 119:105 says, "Your word is a lamp to my feet and a light to my path" *(The Amplified Bible).*

When you sin against your brother, not only do you break fellowship

with him but you do not enjoy good
fellowship with the Father. You
have broken the law of love and are
not living in and doing the truth.
Darkness begins to blind your eyes.
Your decisions will not be accurate
because you have stepped out of
The WORD, out of light, out of

FEAR HAS NO PLACE
IN LOVE BECAUSE
FEAR COMES FROM
SELFISHNESS.

fellowship, and out of love into darkness. As long as you operate in love,
you continue in the light as He is in the light.

First John 2:9-11 says:

> He that saith he is in the light, and hateth his brother, is
> in darkness even until now. He that loveth his brother
> abideth in the light, and there is none occasion of stum-
> bling in him. But he that hateth his brother is in dark-
> ness, and walketh in darkness, and knoweth not whither
> he goeth, because that darkness hath blinded his eyes.

When you practice love toward your brother, you are abiding in the
light and there is no occasion for stumbling or error. You will make the right
decisions, know the will of God and be in close fellowship with the Father.

Selfishness is the opposite of the love that does not seek its own. It
is the open door to ruin. Every sin is selfish. You do not sin for someone
else. No man or woman ever committed adultery for his neighbor. Every
word of retaliation to insult or hurt comes in an effort to protect oneself.
Every cutting word said is for your own advantage or satisfaction.

Selfishness demands its own rights and its own way. It works in
order to protect and promote the big "me." It is sin. Resist it just as you
would resist lying or stealing (both of which also stem from selfishness—all sins do).

Since you have learned what the love of God is and how it works, you will better understand the force of selfishness and how to detect it. Every action that is opposed to the love of God as defined in 1 Corinthians 13:4-8 is selfishness.

Just as faith works by love, fear works by selfishness. Fear's torment is, *"What is going to happen to me?"* Selfishness is the foundation of fear—fear of failure, fear of people, fear of sickness, fear of poverty, fear of being cheated, fear of losing, fear of harm, fear of death. *Fear hath torment.*

First John 4:18 says, "There is no fear in love; but perfect love casteth out fear: because fear hath torment. He that feareth is not made perfect in love."

Perfect love has no fear because love casts out fear. Love's peace says, "What can I do for you?" not, "What are you going to do to me?" Love does not seek its own. Therefore it is not afraid of being hurt or mistreated. Fear has no place in love because fear comes from selfishness.

Love gives—selfishness takes. Love has peace—fear has torment. Love causes success—fear causes failure. God Is Love. Satan is selfishness.

Satan's nature is selfish and his children are in his likeness. The world is full of selfish, unlovely, greedy and hateful people who move at his command. These unlovely ones are the cross we have to bear, but we are to love them as Jesus loves them.

When you act out of love, be quick to confess it to the Father in the Name of Jesus and receive forgiveness according to 1 John 1:9. If you get into darkness, don't allow yourself to stay there. Get your fellowship restored with the Father and with your brother.

By confessing your sins you are once again abiding in the light—unless you continue to hold resentment or bitterness. Resentment and bitterness have to go when you confess the sin. When you ask forgiveness and use 1 Corinthians 13:4-8, applying all that love is to your situation, you are enforcing the *agape* love that never fails, and have returned to the light.

ENEMIES OF LOVE

"For the whole Law [concerning human relationships] is complied with in the one precept, You shall love your neighbor as [you do] your-self. But if you bite and devour one another [in partisan strife], be careful that you [and your whole fellowship] are not consumed by one another" (Galatians 5:14-15, *The Amplified Bible*).

Love has many enemies—envy, anger, hatred, pride, slander, wrath, bitterness, malice, clamor and unforgiveness. These enemies of love all produce strife, and all come from selfishness. They are fiery darts Satan uses to rob believers of spiritual power and influence.

Satan uses these weapons in an attempt to convince the world that Christianity is just another religion. (Remember, Jesus said in John 13:35, "By this shall all men know that ye are my disciples, if you have love one to another.")

Satan begins to gain mastery over believers the moment they step out of love, drawing them into the realm of selfishness and darkness where he can work. In that realm, the believer is rendered powerless. When you walk out of the spirit and by the senses, you are no threat to him.

He uses strife, a powerful force, to hinder the work of the Body of Christ, which then paralyzes revival in the earth. Believers cannot oper-ate in love and be in strife with one another.

If you bite and devour one another in strife, your family, brethren or whole fellowship can be consumed. The power of agreement is then stopped. Jesus said, "Again I say unto you, That if two of you shall agree on earth as touching any thing that they shall ask, it shall be done for them of my Father which is in heaven. For where two or three are gathered together in my name, there am I in the midst of them" (Matthew 18:19-20).

There is great power in agreement between the brethren—a man and wife, or any two of you. Jesus said that whatever you agree on and ask for will come to pass. He is in the midst of you to carry out that agreement.

Ken and I have learned through The WORD to live in agreement with each other. The power of harmony is at work in our lives—whatever we agree on, according to God's WORD, comes to pass. We do not allow strife in our home, office or any part of our ministry. It stops the power of God!

Kenneth and I have learned a great truth: It is more important to avoid strife than to appear justified! It is better to give than to receive, and the wisdom from above is peace-loving and easily entreated, willing to yield to reason. As a result, we are enjoying one of God's greatest blessings—a love-ruled home.

When you begin to order your life by the love of God, you will find the easiest place to remain in selfishness is in your own home with those dearest to you. There seems to be an incentive to operate in love with those outside your family. But, at home, you are tempted to allow yourself more selfish privileges—as if selfishness did not really count there. There are no constraints in the home to keep you from seeking your own except the love of God. Before you even thought about living the love of God, you were probably more courteous and just nicer in many ways to friends than to your family. Without the love of God, you are more demanding and less forgiving with the members of your family than with anyone else. It doesn't make sense, but most of the time, you will say things to those close to you that you wouldn't dream of saying to other people.

Strife and selfishness are luxuries Christians cannot afford—especially at home! *If you allow Satan to stop you with strife at your own front door, you will be no threat to him anywhere else.* The home is where strife is the deadliest, and the home is also the place where living the love of God produces the greatest joy and blessing. Your home will become a copy of heaven on earth when it is love-ruled by The WORD of God.

A Christian husband and wife who learn to live in agreement—without strife—are mighty instruments of The LORD Jesus for good. The rewards of living in agreement are more than worth the effort it takes to walk in love with each other.

Discord or disagreement—strife—between the brethren, between a man and wife, or between any two of you drops the shield of faith, stops prayer results, and invites Satan and his evil spirits into the midst of you.

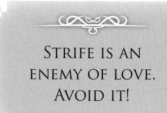

STRIFE IS AN ENEMY OF LOVE. AVOID IT!

> But if ye have bitter envying and strife in your hearts, glory not, and lie not against the truth. This wisdom descendeth not from above, but is earthly, sensual, devilish. For where envying and strife is, there is confusion and every evil work. But the wisdom that is from above is first pure, then peaceable, gentle, and easy to be intreated, full of mercy and good fruits, without partiality, and without hypocrisy (James 3:14-17).

Envy results in strife. Envy (jealousy) and strife (contention, rivalry and selfish ambition) are areas of darkness. Strife opens the door to every evil work and brings confusion. When you walk in strife, you walk in a devilish wisdom—the wisdom of darkness where your senses will dominate your spirit. It will stop you from perfecting the love of God and will keep you from walking in the light of His wisdom.

Strife is deadly. The moment you become aware of Satan trying to move you into it, stop it immediately with the Name of Jesus. Learn to resist it just as you learned to resist sin and sickness. *Stop contention!* It proceeds from Satan. Philippians 2:3 says, "Let nothing be done through strife or vainglory." Obey God's WORD, and be free from Satan's evil works.

Selfishness produces strife. Love produces peace. God's wisdom is pure, peaceable, gentle and easily entreated. It is full of mercy and good fruits, without partiality and without hypocrisy (James 3:17).

Strife is an enemy of love. Avoid it!

Study and meditate on what God's wisdom says about strife in the Proverbs of Solomon:

> Hatred stirreth up strifes: but love covereth all sins (Proverbs 10:12).

> Only by pride cometh contention: but with the well advised is wisdom (Proverbs 13:10).

> A wrathful man stirreth up strife: but he that is slow to anger appeaseth strife (Proverbs 15:18).

> A froward man[14] soweth strife: and a whisperer separateth chief friends (Proverbs 16:28).

> He who is slow to anger is better than the mighty, he who rules his [own] spirit than he who takes a city (Proverbs 16:32, *The Amplified Bible*).

> Better is a dry morsel with quietness than a house full of feasting [on offered sacrifices] with strife (Proverbs 17:1, *The Amplified Bible*).

> The beginning of strife is as when water first trickles [from a crack in a dam]; therefore stop contention before it becomes worse and quarreling breaks out (Proverbs 17:14, *The Amplified Bible*).

> He loveth transgression that loveth strife: and he that

---

14 Synonyms for *froward:* unyielding, perverse, disobedient, ungovernable, cross, peevish

exalteth his gate seeketh destruction (Proverbs 17:19).

It is an honour for a man to cease from strife: but every fool will be meddling (Proverbs 20:3).

He who, passing by, stops to meddle with strife that is none of his business is like one who takes a dog by the ears (Proverbs 26:17, *The Amplified Bible*).

Where no wood is, there the fire goeth out: so where there is no talebearer, the strife ceaseth. As coals are to burning coals, and wood to fire; so is a contentious man to kindle strife (Proverbs 26:20-21).

He who is of a greedy spirit stirs up strife, but he who puts his trust in The LORD shall be enriched and BLESSED (Proverbs 28:25, *The Amplified Bible*).

An angry man stirreth up strife, and a furious man aboundeth in transgression (Proverbs 29:22).

Surely the churning of milk bringeth forth butter, and the wringing of the nose bringeth forth blood: so the forcing of wrath bringeth forth strife (Proverbs 30:33).

CORRUPT COMMUNICATION

Neither give place to the devil.... Let no corrupt communication proceed out of your mouth, but that which is good to the use of edifying, that it may minister grace unto the hearers. And grieve not the holy Spirit of God, whereby ye are sealed unto the day of redemption. Let all bitterness, and wrath, and anger, and clamour [quarreling], and evil

speaking [slander], be put away from you, with all malice
[ill will] (Ephesians 4:27, 29-31).

Call these enemies of love out loud by name and command them, in
the Name of Jesus, to get out of your life. (Other enemies of love are listed
in Galatians 5:19-21.) Many are active evil spirits assigned to keep you
in strife. Hatred, pride, whispering, anger, meddling and wrath are open
doors to strife, and through these, the believer gives place to Satan. Give
no place to the devil. Resist him and he will flee from you (James 4:7).

Corrupt communication causes strife and does damage to you and to
others. Notice that all these enemies of love are turned loose by the tongue.
We are admonished to speak only what is good, edifying and that ministers
grace, or blessing, to the hearer. James describes a fully developed character
and a perfect man as one who does not offend in speech (James 3:2, *The
Amplified Bible*). By using good and beneficial speech, we neither give place
to the devil, nor do we grieve the Holy Spirit.

Instruct your mouth to use words that edify or build up the hearer.
Become conscious of words that minister grace.

"Let there be no filthiness (obscenity, indecency) nor foolish
and sinful (silly and corrupt) talk, nor coarse jesting, which are not
fitting or becoming; but instead voice your thankfulness [to God]"
(Ephesians 5:4, *The Amplified Bible*).

The LORD not only tells us to stop all corrupt communication
but also instructs us in what we *are* to speak: Instead of voicing corrupt
communication, *voice your thankfulness to God.* Replace evil speaking and
words of strife with the praise of God. The Scripture also teaches about
the power of praise.

Psalm 9:2-3 says, "I will be glad and rejoice in thee: I will sing praise
to thy name, O thou most High. When mine enemies are turned back,
they shall fall and perish at thy presence."

Psalm 8:2 says, "Out of the mouth of babes and sucklings hast thou ordained strength because of thine enemies, that thou mightest still the enemy and the avenger."

Jesus, in quoting this scripture in Matthew 21:16, said, "Out of the mouth of babes and sucklings thou hast perfected praise." Praise stills the enemy and the avenger!

Psalm 22:3 says God inhabits the praises of His people. Praise also brings the presence of God on the scene. The enemy turns back, falls and perishes at His presence.

We are instructed to forgive one another even as God has forgiven us—freely, unconditionally—with grace (undeserved favor) and blessing: "And be ye kind one to another, tenderhearted, forgiving one another, even as God for Christ's sake hath forgiven you" (Ephesians 4:32).

First Corinthians 13:5 tells us that love "takes no account of the evil done to it [it pays no attention to a suffered wrong]" *(The Amplified Bible)*. Jesus said, "But I say unto you, Love your enemies, bless them that curse you, do good to them that hate you, and pray for them which despitefully use you, and persecute you; that ye may be the children of your Father which is in heaven" (Matthew 5:44-45).

Unforgiveness, like strife, is a thief that comes to steal, kill and destroy. If you are not acting in the love of God, the things that people do or say to you can hurt you. If you resent and hold an offense against another, it injures *you*. It holds *you* in bondage and renders your prayer life powerless.

Luke 6:37 says, "Judge not, and ye shall not be judged: condemn not, and ye shall not be condemned: forgive, and ye shall be forgiven." In *Vine's Expository Dictionary of Biblical Words*, the Greek word translated *forgive*, in this verse, means "to loose from, to release."[15] This scripture is saying, "Loose, and you will be loosed."

---

15 *Vine's Expository Dictionary of Biblical Words*, W.E. Vine, Merrill F. Unger, William White (ed.) (Nashville: Thomas Nelson Publishers, 1985) "forgive, forgave, forgiveness," p. 251.

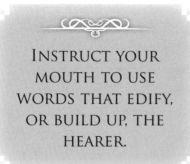

INSTRUCT YOUR
MOUTH TO USE
WORDS THAT EDIFY,
OR BUILD UP, THE
HEARER.

When you forgive as God forgives, you let that person go free from the transgression. You release him from guilt, *unconditionally.* You let go of any resentment against him. It is as though it never happened. You refuse to hold anything against him, even if Satan continues to bring it to your mind. No doubt, he will. Paul told the Corinthians to forgive lest Satan gain the advantage over them (2 Corinthians 2:7-11). *Unforgiveness gives Satan the advantage.* Refuse to dwell on the transgression in your thought life again because you have forgiven the person as God has forgiven you.

Do as Jesus admonished in Mark 11:25-26: "And when ye stand praying, forgive, if ye have ought against any: that your Father also which is in heaven may forgive you your trespasses. But if ye do not forgive, neither will your Father which is in heaven forgive your trespasses."

You forgive as an act of your will. Jesus said to forgive when you stand praying. You cannot stand for a month or even for a week. When you forgive, you give up resentment against another—that only takes a moment. You are forgiving in obedience to God, acting in faith on His WORD.

When you refuse to forgive, you close the door to your own forgiveness from the Father. But when you forgive, you will be forgiven.

Confess the sin of unforgiveness in this manner:

Father, in the Name of Jesus, I confess the sin of unforgiveness. I forgive everyone their trespasses against me. I forgive (call the names out to God that come into your mind). I let go of all resentment toward them right now.

> I hereby loose them from that offense. As I forgive, I
> believe I receive Your forgiveness now.

By confessing the sin of unforgiveness, you have not only freed the other person, but you have also cleansed and freed yourself from unforgiveness, strife and the other enemies of love. Now that you recognize the evil works of these tools of Satan, refuse to give them place in your life.

"Having therefore these promises, dearly beloved, let us *cleanse ourselves* from all filthiness of the flesh and spirit, perfecting holiness in the fear of God" (2 Corinthians 7:1).

Stay cleansed and allow the love of God to work in you, unhindered. Second Timothy 2:20-21 says, "But in a great house there are not only vessels of gold and of silver, but also of wood and of earth; and some to honour, and some to dishonour. If a man therefore *purge himself* from these, he shall be a vessel unto honour, sanctified, and meet for the master's use, and prepared unto every good work."

BEING LED BY THE SPIRIT

> And let the peace (soul harmony which comes) from
> Christ rule (act as umpire continually) in your hearts
> [deciding and settling with finality all questions that
> arise in your minds, in that peaceful state] to which as
> [members of Christ's] one body you were also called [to
> live]. And be thankful (appreciative), [giving praise to
> God always] (Colossians 3:15, *The Amplified Bible*).

> For as many as are led by the Spirit of God, they are the
> sons of God (Romans 8:14).

In making decisions concerning the specific will of God for your life, learn from Colossians 3:15 how to recognize the leading, or inward witness, of the Spirit. This witness comes from your spirit into your mind. It is described as the peace in your heart. The heart of man is the spirit of man.

"The spirit of man is the candle of The LORD, searching all the inward parts of the belly" (Proverbs 20:27). The Holy Spirit lives in your spirit. This is where His guidance will come from. The spirit of man is where the light of The LORD reveals guidance and answers to God's children.

God speaks to you through your spirit. "The Spirit itself [himself] beareth witness with our spirit, that we are the children of God" (Romans 8:16). The inward witness concerning the affairs of life is the same Spirit bearing witness with your spirit and gives you peace about salvation, assuring you that you are a child of God.

This peace is to act as an umpire in your heart. One definition of *umpire* is "something that decides a matter." As you meditate and pray over the matter, this peace or inward witness of the heart will tell you yes or no, stop or go ahead. If you are agitated in your spirit, there is no peace, and something (your spirit) tells you that things are not right. *Stop!* Go no further in that direction.

On the other hand, if you have peace or the inward witness that says it is right, then go ahead. The Holy Spirit will give you an inward peace or witness about the thing that God would have you to do. Expect the Holy Spirit to make the will of God real to you.

The WORD says that the sons of God are to be led by the Spirit of God. The ministry of the Holy Spirit includes guiding you in the affairs of life. Expect His guidance.

Do not go against what you have peace about in your heart. Follow your spirit. Let the peace decide and settle, with finality, any and all questions.

If you get into an area of indecision, and do not recognize the inward witness either way, *do nothing.* Be still and know that He is God. Get

in The WORD and pray in the
spirit—in tongues—until you
know what God wants. Many times
in this area of indecision, Satan will
try to push you and tell you that
you *have* to do something *now* even
if it is wrong. He is a liar and the
truth is not in him. You do not have
to do anything until peace settles the issue in your heart.

> LET PEACE DECIDE
> AND SETTLE, WITH
> FINALITY, ANY AND
> ALL QUESTIONS.

The Holy Spirit will lead you primarily by the inward witness, but the
voice of The LORD may also come to you. It will be stronger and clearer
than the inward witness and you will surely recognize it when He speaks.

The LORD also speaks to His people by His prophets, and through
visions and dreams. Spiritual gifts are still in operation in the Church. In
the New Testament, we have record of The LORD sending His angel to
lead and guide. For example, the angel of The LORD spoke to Philip and
told him to go to Gaza (Acts 8:26). All these avenues of receiving guidance are subject to God's WORD. If any guidance comes to you that is
not in line with The WORD, *disregard it.*

You have already learned that God's will is His WORD. The Holy
Spirit will never lead you contrary to The WORD. The Spirit and The
WORD agree. *Always judge guidance by The WORD.*

When you take the time to learn God's will in His WORD, you
will be able to know and recognize the voice of your spirit guided by the
Holy Spirit. Determine to fulfill God's will for you, and God will see to it
that you know His guidance.

SCRIPTURE:

"A new commandment I give unto you, That ye love one another; as I have loved you, that ye also love one another. By this shall all men know that ye are my disciples, if ye have love one to another" (John 13:34-35).

POINTS TO REMEMBER:

1. What an honor the Father has bestowed upon you—the ability and the right to love and be loved *with His love.* You are the open door into the love of God for the people with whom you come in contact.

2. To walk in God is to walk in the light. To walk in the light is to walk in The WORD. To walk in The WORD is to walk in love. To walk in love is to walk in the spirit. To walk in the spirit is to walk in wisdom. To walk in wisdom is to walk in success. And to walk in success is to walk in God.

3. Love gives—selfishness takes. Love has peace—fear has torment. Love causes success—fear causes failure. God Is Love.

CONFESSION:

I keep myself in the kingdom of light, in love and in The WORD, and the wicked one touches me not. Therefore I declare from 1 Corinthians 13:4-8 *(The Amplified Bible),* that I endure long and I am patient and kind. I never am envious, nor do I boil over with jealousy. I am not boastful or vainglorious, nor do I display myself haughtily. I am not conceited (arrogant or inflated with pride). I am not rude or unmannerly, nor do I act unbecomingly. Love (God's love in me) does not insist on its own rights or its own way, for I am not self-seeking. I am not touchy, fretful or resentful. I take no account of the evil done to me, I pay no attention to a suffered wrong. I do not rejoice at injustice or unrighteousness, but I rejoice when right and truth prevail. I bear up under anything and everything that comes, I am ever ready to believe the best of every person. My hopes are fadeless under all circumstances, and I endure everything without weakening. I never fail because God's love in me never fades out or becomes obsolete or comes to an end.

CHAPTER SIX

God's Will Is Prosperity

I t is obvious, throughout the Bible, that God is not against a man having money or being prosperous. God's covenant men were the wealthiest men of their day. They were God's men, and He was pleased with them. Their attitude toward God's WORD allowed Him to establish His covenant with them in their generations. God is the One who gave them the power to get wealth. "But you shall [earnestly] remember The LORD your God; for it is He Who gives you power to get wealth, that He may establish His covenant which He swore to your fathers, as it is this day" (Deuteronomy 8:18, *The Amplified Bible*).

God is not against a man having money. He is against money having the man. He is not opposed to His people being rich, but He is opposed to their being covetous.

WHERE IS YOUR TRUST?

Jesus said to not gather, heap up and store for yourselves treasure on

GOD IS NOT AGAINST A MAN HAVING MONEY. HE IS AGAINST MONEY HAVING THE MAN.

earth. In Luke 12:16-21, He speaks of the man who continues to lay up or hoard possessions for himself and is not rich toward God. To hoard is not of God. This man was not remembering that it was God who had given him the power to get wealth. (Your affection is not to be toward your prosperity, business, goods, treasures or holdings.) Jesus said this rich man had fertile land which yielded so plentifully that it put him in a dilemma. *All* of his storehouses were full, and he did not have room to store another big harvest, so he decided to tear down his storehouses and build bigger ones: "Now, I have good things laid up for many years. I can just live the way I want to." His trust was in the things he had laid up, the things he had hoarded!

"But God said to him, You fool! This very night they...demand your soul of you; and all the things that you have prepared, whose will they be? So it is with the one who continues to lay up and hoard possessions for himself and is not rich...to God [this is how he fares]" (Luke 12:20-21, *The Amplified Bible*).

Trusting in riches will go only as far as the riches will go, but God's prosperity reaches into every area of a person's life.

PROSPERITY IS

True prosperity is the ability to use the power of God to meet the needs of mankind. If a man needs healing, money will not help him. If his body is well but he has no money to pay the rent, God's healing power will not cover his need. God is so generous with us that He desires His children to have the best in life on earth, just as you desire the best for your children. God's plan for us is to have *all* our needs met according to His riches in glory by Christ Jesus. True prosperity is having every need met.

God's laws of prosperity carry with them a built-in protection. For His laws of prosperity to work in your life, you must be spiritually ready to prosper. Throughout the Bible, God's people prospered when they obeyed His WORD. When they were disobedient, His laws of prosperity did not work for them. They were still His people, but His powerful BLESSING

GOD'S PROSPERITY REACHES INTO EVERY AREA OF A PERSON'S LIFE.

was not manifest in their lives. "Keep therefore the words of this covenant, and do them, that ye may prosper in all that ye do" (Deuteronomy 29:9). God does not change. The laws of prosperity will work in the life of any person who is obedient to His WORD.

You will not prosper by believing only the part of God's WORD concerning material blessing. Your motive for becoming prosperous must be to serve God and meet the needs of others. God's prosperity will work only in the life of the believer who is committed to The WORD because he loves God—not just to get something for himself.

YOUR FIRST PRIORITY

Your first priority must be to please God. For where your treasure is, there will your heart be also. If your treasure is Jesus and His WORD, then you are a candidate for the material BLESSING of God.

As we discussed in a previous chapter, in Matthew 6:22, Jesus explains the saying "The light of the body is the eye." You must have your priorities in the right place so when you begin to enjoy material prosperity, you will keep your priorities in line.

If your affection is set on wealth and riches instead of God, The WORD will become unfruitful in your life. Covetousness chokes The WORD. The WORD cannot bear fruit in a man who has his affections and priorities set on the things of the earth. The successful faith man sets his mind (affection) on The WORD of God. You cannot serve God and mammon (verse 24).

The choice is yours. Either you trust in mammon (deceitful riches, money, possessions) or you trust in God. If your trust is in mammon, when you are instructed by God to give a large amount into His work, for example, you will give a small amount, instead. You'll think, *I would like to give more, but it is all tied up*. You are serving riches. That is where you have placed your faith.

But, if your eye is single on God's WORD and He instructs you to give, you will say to The LORD, "You know my money is tied up, but at Your instruction, I will untie it!"

The man whose eye is single on The WORD has confidence in The LORD. He knows that when he gives, it shall be given to him again— good measure, pressed down, shaken together and running over (Luke 6:38). He is not hoarding. He is ready to distribute as God tells him. He is not trusting in his riches, but has confidence in God's ability to put him over. He is not serving money. Money is his servant.

Serving God, and not money, is the highest priority of a prosperous man. Make this *your* highest priority today by making a quality decision—a decision of no return—to set your eyes on Jesus, and not on "things."

True Prosperity

Third John 2 says, "Beloved, I wish above all things that thou mayest prosper and be in health, even as thy soul prospereth" (3 John 2). To be prosperous, you must first have a prosperous soul. But how do you get there?

As I mentioned earlier in the book, my journey to the prosperous life began years ago when I first read Matthew 6:33 in a Bible Ken's mother had given him: "But seek ye first the kingdom of God, and his righteousness; and all these things shall be added unto you." In *The Amplified Bible* it says to seek *"His way of doing and being right."* That's the foundation of God's prosperity. When I found that verse, I was ready to try God's way, since I needed a lot of things and my way wasn't working!

I discovered that God's prosperity isn't just financial BLESSING. It also includes healing, protection, favor, wisdom, success, well-being and every good thing you could possibly need—all the good things Jesus paid for you to have.

He took our place and bore the curse of our sin so we can live in THE BLESSING. Galatians 3:13-14 says, "Christ hath redeemed us from the curse of the law, being made a curse for us: for it is written, Cursed is every one that hangeth on a tree: That THE BLESSING of Abraham might come on the Gentiles through Jesus Christ...." Isaiah 53:5 says, "The chastisement [needful to obtain] peace and well-being for us was upon Him, and with the stripes [that wounded] Him we are healed and made whole" *(The Amplified Bible)*. The Hebrew word for *peace* in this scripture is *shalom.* It basically means "nothing missing, nothing broken," or wholeness in every area of your life—spirit, soul and body.

That kind of prosperous life doesn't just happen. And it doesn't happen overnight. But the foundation for true prosperity begins with these seven principles:

1. *Walking in truth*

2. *Faithfulness*

3. *Diligence*

4. *Tithing*

5. *Sowing*

6. *Believing*

7. *Saying*

Let's briefly take a look at each one of these key elements to walking in prosperity.

WALKING IN TRUTH

Third John 4 says, "I have no greater joy than to hear that my children walk in truth." (If I were to tell you about heaven, I couldn't give you any firsthand information because I haven't been there. But, when I teach on prosperity, that's something I have experienced from minus zero to abundance. Kenneth and I have been walking in the laws of abundance for many years.)

As I told you, we weren't exactly walking in prosperity when we married. I wore a $2 veil with the white cotton dress my mother made for the wedding. Ken's friend married us at his home. His wife baked a cake. We even borrowed $100 for our honeymoon. We had no money and no wisdom. You would be hard-pressed to find a couple more pitifully ignorant than we were at that time.

But then, something happened that totally changed our lives. We began to hear the truth of The WORD of God. First we were born again. We were changed inside, but outwardly you still couldn't tell much difference in us. Then, we were filled with the Holy Spirit. There was some outward change, but we were still ignorant of The WORD. The real changes in our lives came when we started walking on The WORD and letting the wisdom of God become our way of life. Everything began to change!

We found the first step to increase is *walking in truth*. That means walking in the light of God's WORD, according to His ways, His wisdom, what He says is right. You can't do that and not be BLESSED. Jesus said, "If ye continue in my WORD, then are ye my disciples indeed; and ye shall know the truth, and the truth shall make you free" (John 8:31-32).

I'm not just talking about reading scriptures about prosperity. You prosper when you walk in all the words God says to you. That's the wisdom of God.

Walking in truth is living a godly lifestyle—living in obedience to what God says is right. THE BLESSING God outlined in Deuteronomy 28:1-14 will manifest as a result of obedience. "And it shall come to pass,

GOD DESIRES FOR YOU TO LIVE WITHIN HIS CIRCLE OF BLESSING.

if thou shalt hearken diligently unto the voice of The LORD thy God, to observe and to do all his commandments which I command thee this day, that The LORD thy God will set thee on high above all nations of the earth: And all these BLESSINGS shall come on thee, and overtake thee..." (verses 1-2).

God has always BLESSED an obedient people. Isaiah 1:19 says, "If ye be willing and obedient, ye shall eat the good of the land." God can do something with a person who has a willing heart. Psalm 25:12-13 in *The Living Bible* promises that when you fear The LORD, "God will teach [you] how to choose the best. [You] shall live within God's circle of BLESSING."

One of the first things God taught us was to stay out of debt—and we obeyed Him! That was big to us in those days. We started where we were, and that meant believing God to pay the overdue bills. But increase came as we were willing and obedient to walk in the truth of The WORD.

And, increase can come to you, too. God desires for you to live within His circle of BLESSING. It is His will for you to increase.

FAITHFULNESS AND DILIGENCE

In Matthew 25:21, Jesus said of the faithful servant: "His lord said unto him, Well done, thou good and faithful servant: thou hast been faithful over a few things, I will make thee ruler over many things: enter thou into the joy of thy lord."

The force of faithfulness is a fruit of the spirit that you received when you were born again. Webster's dictionary defines *faithful* as "full of faith, believing, strong or firm in one's faith, firmly adhering to duty, a true fidelity, loyal, true to allegiance, constant in the performance of duties or services."

A faithful person consistently does what is right, even if it looks like it could be to his disadvantage. Psalm 106:3 says, "BLESSED are they who maintain justice, who constantly do what is right" *(New International Version-*84).

Faithfulness is God's character:

> It is because of The LORD's mercy and loving-kindness that we are not consumed, because His [tender] compassions fail not. They are new every morning; great and abundant is Your stability and faithfulness (Lamentations 3:22-23, *The Amplified Bible*).

> God is faithful (reliable, trustworthy, and therefore ever true to His promise, and He can be depended on); by Him you were called into companionship and participation with His Son, Jesus Christ our LORD (1 Corinthians 1:9, *The Amplified Bible*).

Second Chronicles 16:9 says God is looking for faithfulness, "For the eyes of The LORD run to and fro throughout the whole earth, to show himself strong in the behalf of them whose heart is perfect toward him...." The Hebrew word for *perfect* there can also mean "faithful."

Kenneth and I have had financial trouble, challenges with sickness and other things, but when we have stood on The WORD and refused to give up, God has always been faithful to answer our faith with His action!

Once you find a promise in His WORD, don't disqualify yourself from receiving by saying, "God would never do that for me." Be transformed by the renewing of your mind (Romans 12:2). Let God's WORD change your thinking. You will prosper in any area as your soul [mind,

THE NO. 1 LAW
OF RECEIVING IS
DON'T QUIT!

will and emotions] prospers in understanding about that area from The WORD, and you take that knowledge and act on it. Your inner man prospers when you believe The WORD. Your circumstances prosper when you receive what He says and act on it.

Be faithful to keep meditating the promises in The WORD until they overtake your life. Everything you receive from God starts with The WORD in your heart. Proverbs 4:20-23 says, "My son, attend to my words; incline thine ear unto my sayings. Let them not depart from thine eyes; keep them in the midst of thine heart. For they are life unto those that find them, and health to all their flesh. Keep thy heart with all diligence; for out of it are the issues of life."

Faithfulness will energize you to be diligent even if you have never been that way in the natural. The WORD repeatedly says we are to *diligently* seek God, hearken to what He says and obey His commands. Why? Deuteronomy 28:1-2 says when you hearken diligently, THE BLESSING overtakes you! "...He is a rewarder of them that diligently seek him" (Hebrews 11:6). Diligence increases you. As Proverbs 10:4 says, "The hand of the diligent maketh rich."

Be diligent and faithful to God in your natural life, as well. Make the decision to be faithful on your job, at your church, in your prayer life and in putting The WORD first place in your life.

Our souls prosper as we spend time in The WORD, believe it and create a lifestyle of obeying God. The result will be what 1 John 3:22 says: "And we receive from Him whatever we ask, because we [watchfully] obey His orders [observe His suggestions and injunctions, follow His plan for us] and [habitually] practice what is pleasing to Him" *(The Amplified Bible)*.

The No. 1 law of receiving is *don't quit!* Stay with The WORD. Stay with what God has told you to do. Even if you make a mistake, repent and get back on track. That's faithfulness. It's part of the prosperous life because "a faithful man shall abound with BLESSINGS..." (Proverbs 28:20).

Tithing and Sowing

Proverbs 3:9-10 says, "Honor The LORD with your capital and sufficiency...and with the firstfruits of all your income; so shall your storage places be filled with plenty, and your vats shall be overflowing with new wine" *(The Amplified Bible).*

Ken and I never had any financial growth until we became faithful in tithing. At first it looked impossible to give that 10 percent. But when we did, the 90 percent we had left went further than the 100 percent we had before.

Tithing is a covenant transaction that gets God involved in what you are doing. The first 10 percent of your income—the tithe—belongs to God. The Bible calls it firstfruits. It's devoted to God, and it goes to support ministries that feed you spiritually.

Tithing is how you honor God with your money. It makes a way for God's supernatural BLESSING in your life.

Notice Malachi 3:10 says to bring *all* the tithes to God. It also says by doing so, God will open the windows of heaven and BLESS you so "that there shall not be room to receive it!" You don't want to keep anything that belongs to God. Leviticus 27:30 declares, "And all the tithe of the land, whether of the seed of the land, or of the fruit of the tree, is The LORD's: it is holy unto The LORD."

Real tithing is done with the heart and with the mouth, in faith. God commanded His people to bring their firstfruits: "And thou shalt set it before The LORD thy God, and worship before The LORD thy God: And thou shalt rejoice in every good thing which The LORD thy God hath given unto thee, and unto thine house..." (Deuteronomy 26:10-11). The people were to recount how God had delivered them out of bondage. They

> TITHING IS
> A COVENANT
> TRANSACTION THAT
> GETS GOD INVOLVED
> IN WHAT YOU
> ARE DOING.

were to worship Him and rejoice for all the good He had given them.

Whatever we do must be in obedience and in faith for God to be pleased with it.

Everything we do toward God must come from our hearts, otherwise it doesn't count. Jesus said, "It is the spirit that quickeneth; the flesh profiteth nothing..." (John 6:63). We are to give with a willing heart, as an honor to God, and worship Him with our tithes. Then He is in partnership with us.

After we tithe, we are to sow according to what The LORD lays on our heart, and we are to do it with the right attitude. The Hebrew word for offering comes from a root word that means to "draw nigh." We draw nigh to God with our offering. Second Corinthians 9:6 says: "He which soweth sparingly shall reap also sparingly; and he which soweth bountifully shall reap also bountifully."

The Scripture plainly says you reap what you sow (Galatians 6:7). If you desire to be a receiver, you have to be a giver. "Give, and it shall be given unto you; good measure, pressed down, and shaken together, and running over, shall men give into your bosom. For with the same measure that ye mete withal it shall be measured to you again" (Luke 6:38).

Tithing is supernatural—don't miss out on the benefits. God has an interest in your finances—He desires to increase you and BLESS you because He loves you.

BELIEVING AND SAYING

Second Corinthians 4:13 says, "We having the same spirit of faith, according as it is written, I believed, and therefore have I spoken; we also believe, and therefore speak."

The Bible says several times, "The just shall live by faith" (Romans 1:17; Galatians 3:11; Hebrews 10:38). Abraham was BLESSED because he lived by faith. He believed God. We're supposed to live the same way: "So then they which be of faith are BLESSED with faithful Abraham" (Galatians 3:9).

Faith must be in two places—in your heart and in your mouth. "The WORD is nigh thee, even in thy mouth, and in thy heart: that is, The WORD of faith, which we preach" (Romans 10:8). Believing in your heart and saying with your mouth produce the operation of faith.

"For verily I say unto you, That whosoever shall say unto this mountain, Be thou removed, and be thou cast into the sea; and shall not doubt in his heart, but shall believe that those things which he saith shall come to pass; he shall have whatsoever he saith" (Mark 11:23).

Kenneth and I learned to take The WORD literally as God speaking to us. We learned if we put it in our eyes, put it in our ears, and let it get down into our hearts in abundance, it would come out of our mouths in faith-filled words that would change our lives and circumstances.

We realized all that stood between us and walking in the dream God had for us was knowing what is in the Book and doing it. Joshua was told: "This book of the law shall not depart out of thy mouth; but thou shalt meditate therein day and night, that thou mayest observe to do according to all that is written therein: for then thou shalt make thy way prosperous, and then thou shalt have good success" (Joshua 1:8).

The seven keys I've shared are how Ken and I laid a foundation for the prosperous life—and this is how we maintain it. I can tell you from experience, these are the first seven steps to increase, no matter what you need.

You can live the life of prosperity—it's God's will for you!

SCRIPTURE:

"But seek (aim at and strive after) first of all His kingdom and His righteousness (His way of doing and being right), and then all these things taken together will be given you besides" (Matthew 6:33, *The Amplified Bible*).

POINTS TO REMEMBER:

1. God is so generous with us that He desires His children to have the best in life on earth, just as you desire the best for your children. God's plan for us is to have *all* our needs met according to His riches in glory by Christ Jesus. True prosperity is having every need met.

2. The first step to increase is *walking in truth.* That means walking in the light of God's WORD, according to His ways, His wisdom, what He says is right.

3. Faith must be in two places—in your heart and in your mouth. Believing in your heart and saying with your mouth produces the operation of faith.

CONFESSION:

I earnestly remember The LORD my God, for it is He who gives me the power to get wealth, so that He may establish His covenant in my life. I do not trust in uncertain riches, but my trust is in The LORD. I am obedient to His WORD, and I prosper, as my soul prospers, in all that I set my hand to do.

Pleasing God is my first priority. Where my treasure is, there is my heart also. My affections are on The WORD of God. I believe it and speak it in faith. Healing, protection, favor, wisdom, success, well-being and every good thing I could possibly need, are all mine in Jesus. Because I put God's WORD first place, the foundation of true prosperity is laid in my life. I meditate in God's WORD day and night, and I incline my heart to His sayings. They are life to me because I have found them and health to all my flesh. I walk in truth, faithfulness and diligence and do what is right in God's sight. God shows Himself strong in my behalf.

I am a covenant believer, and I am prospering in all I do!

Study the scriptures and reread this book, until who you are in Jesus Christ becomes a reality to you. This reality will become the power and strength of your life!

Prayer for Salvation and Baptism in the Holy Spirit

Heavenly Father, I come to You in the Name of Jesus. Your Word says, "Whosoever shall call on the name of the Lord shall be saved" (Acts 2:21). I am calling on You. I pray and ask Jesus to come into my heart and be Lord over my life according to Romans 10:9-10: "If thou shalt confess with thy mouth the Lord Jesus, and shalt believe in thine heart that God hath raised him from the dead, thou shalt be saved. For with the heart man believeth unto righteousness; and with the mouth confession is made unto salvation." I do that now. I confess that Jesus is Lord, and I believe in my heart that God raised Him from the dead.

I am now reborn! I am a Christian—a child of Almighty God! I am saved! You also said in Your Word, "If ye then, being evil, know how to give good gifts unto your children: HOW MUCH MORE shall your heavenly Father give the Holy Spirit to them that ask him?" (Luke 11:13). I'm also asking You to fill me with the Holy Spirit. Holy Spirit, rise up within me as I praise God. I fully expect to speak with other tongues as You give me the utterance (Acts 2:4). In Jesus' Name. Amen!

Begin to praise God for filling you with the Holy Spirit. Speak those words and syllables you receive—not in your own language, but the language given to you by the Holy Spirit. You have to use your own voice. God will not force you to speak. Don't be concerned with how it sounds. It is a heavenly language!

Continue with the blessing God has given you and pray in the spirit every day.

You are a born-again, Spirit-filled believer. You'll never be the same!

Find a good church that boldly preaches God's Word and obeys it. Become part of a church family who will love and care for you as you love and care for them.

We need to be connected to each other. It increases our strength in God. It's God's plan for us.

Make it a habit to watch the *Believer's Voice of Victory* television broadcast and become a doer of the Word, who is blessed in his doing (James 1:22-25).

About the Author

Gloria Copeland is a noted author and minister of the gospel whose teaching ministry is known throughout the world. Believers worldwide know her through Believers' Conventions, Victory Campaigns, magazine articles, teaching audios and videos, and the daily and Sunday *Believer's Voice of Victory* television broadcast, which she hosts with her husband, Kenneth Copeland. She is known for Healing School, which she began teaching and hosting in 1979 at KCM meetings. Gloria delivers the Word of God and the keys to victorious Christian living to millions of people every year.

Gloria is author of the New York Times best-seller, *God's Master Plan for Your Life* and *Live Long, Finish Strong*, as well as numerous favorites, including *God's Will for You, Walk With God, God's Will Is Prosperity, Hidden Treasures* and *To Know Him*. She has also co-authored several books with her husband, including *Family Promises, Healing Promises* and the best-selling daily devotionals, *From Faith to Faith* and *Pursuit of His Presence*.

She holds an honorary doctorate from Oral Roberts University. In 1994, Gloria was voted Christian Woman of the Year, an honor conferred on women whose example demonstrates outstanding Christian leadership. Gloria is also the co-founder and vice president of Kenneth Copeland Ministries in Fort Worth, Texas.

Learn more about Kenneth Copeland Ministries
by visiting our website at **kcm.org**

Materials to Help You Receive Your Healing
by Gloria Copeland

Books

* And Jesus Healed Them All

  God's Prescription for Divine Health

  God's Will for Your Healing

* Harvest of Health

  Words That Heal (gift book with CD enclosed)

Audio Resources

Be Made Whole—Live Long, Live Healthy

God Is a Good God

God Wants You Well

Healing Confessions (CD and minibook)

Healing School

DVD Resources

Be Made Whole—Live Long, Live Healthy

Know Him As Healer

*Available in Spanish

more help, **more answers,**
MORE OF GOD'S PLAN FOR YOU!

The LifeLine
Series
More than 100,000
copies in print.

Healing & Wellness LifeLine Kit 30-3000 God desires for His people to be healed and stay healed, to live a long, healthy life, free from sickness and disease. Whether you are dealing with a dire diagnosis from a doctor or just desiring to live life to its fullest, Kenneth and Gloria Copeland have a lifesaving message for you in this interactive LifeLine kit.

Building Relationships That Last LifeLine Kit 30-3020 As Christians, our relationships should be rich and rewarding—godly connections that spur us on to great things in God. Whether you need broken relationships repaired or just need to strengthen the ones you have, Kenneth and Gloria Copeland show you how to repair, renew and start *Building Relationships That Last.*

Complete Financial Breakthrough LifeLine Kit 30-3010 God's financial system transcends the national economy, the stock market and any company's layoff plan. And He wants you to take advantage of it...not only for your personal BLESSING, but for the advancement of His kingdom!

How to Get Your Prayers Answered LifeLine Kit 30-3030 James 5:16 says, "The effectual fervent prayer of a righteous man availeth much." And that means you can make a difference! Whether you're new to prayer or want to power up your quiet time like never before, Kenneth and Gloria Copeland will help you move from the basics to being a world-changing prayer warrior. You'll learn not only that God answers prayer, but how to pray His will every time—and believe for the breakthrough you need.

To order these products and view the complete catalog visit us at **kcm.org** or
call 800-600-7395 (inside the U.S.); **817-852-6000** (outside the U.S.)
(7 a.m.-5 p.m. CT)

World Offices
Kenneth Copeland Ministries

For more information about KCM and our products,
please write to the office nearest you:

Kenneth Copeland Ministries
Fort Worth, TX 76192-0001

Kenneth Copeland
Locked Bag 2600
Mansfield Delivery Centre
QUEENSLAND 4122
AUSTRALIA

Kenneth Copeland
Post Office Box 15
BATH
BA1 3XN
U.K.

Kenneth Copeland
Private Bag X 909
FONTAINEBLEAU
2032
REPUBLIC OF SOUTH AFRICA

Kenneth Copeland
PO Box 3111 STN LCD 1
Langley BC V3A 4R3
CANADA

Kenneth Copeland Ministries
Post Office Box 84
L'VIV 79000
UKRAINE

Kenneth Copeland Ministries
Singapore Ltd.
My SingPost Box 880178
Singapore 919191

We're Here for You!®

Join Kenneth and Gloria Copeland and the *Believer's Voice of Victory* broadcasts Monday through Friday and on Sunday each week, and learn how faith in God's Word can take your life from ordinary to extraordinary. This teaching from God's Word is designed to get you where you want to be—*on top!*

You can catch the *Believer's Voice of Victory* broadcast on your local, cable or satellite channels.*

Enjoy inspired teaching and encouragement from Kenneth and Gloria Copeland and guest ministers each month in the *Believer's Voice of Victory* magazine. Also included are real-life testimonies of God's miraculous power and divine intervention in the lives of people just like you!

To receive a FREE subscription to
Believer's Voice of Victory, write to:
Kenneth Copeland Ministries
Fort Worth, TX 76192-0001
Or call: 800-600-7395 (inside the U.S.);
817-852-6000 (outside the U.S.)
Or visit **kcm.org**

If you are writing from outside the U.S., please contact the KCM office nearest you. Addresses for all Kenneth Copeland Ministries offices are listed on the previous page.

* Check your local listings for times and stations in your area.